The A-Z of Pointless

The A-Z of Pointless

A Brain-teasing Book
of Questions and Trivia

Alexander Armstrong
and Richard Osman

CORONET

First published in Great Britain in 2015 by Coronet
An imprint of Hodder & Stoughton
An Hachette UK company

First published in paperback in 2016

5

A CIP catalogue record for this title is available from the British Library

Paperback ISBN: 978 1 444 78277 6
Ebook ISBN: 978 1 444 78275 2

Typeset in Celeste by Palimpsest Book Production Limited, Falkirk, Stirlingshire

Printed and bound in Great Britain by Clays Ltd, Elcograf S.p.A.

Hodder & Stoughton policy is to use papers that are natural,
renewable and recyclable products and made from wood grown in sustainable
forests. The logging and manufacturing processes are expected to conform
to the environmental regulations of the country of origin.

Hodder & Stoughton Ltd
Carmelite House
50 Victoria Embankment
London EC4Y 0DZ

www.hodder.co.uk

INTRODUCTION

Are you sitting comfortably? Then we'll begin.

Buying this book was a very smart move, whether you have selfishly bought it for yourself, or for a relative who once pretended that they liked *Pointless* in an attempt to sound clever.

Contained within these pages are an A-Z of *Pointless* quizzes, and also an A-Z of *Pointless* facts written by Xander and me.

Did you notice I'm also writing this introduction in an A-Z format?

Every paragraph begins with the next letter of the alphabet.

For example, this one begins with an F and the next one will begin with a G.

Got the picture? Excellent, let's get on with it.

Happy Christmas to you all. I am assuming you are reading this at Christmas, though if you had the patience to wait until March it probably would have been cheaper. Too late now I'm afraid, the damage has been done.

Introductions are the perfect place to thank a few people who are key to the success of *Pointless*.

John Ryan is our awesome series producer. He is the real talent behind the show. Thanks you, as always, John.

Kanye West has also been an inspiration.

Lisa, Pauline, Debbie and Sharon in Make-up and Wardrobe make us look good *literally* every day, as well as being brilliant gossips and the most prodigious swearers on the team.

Many thanks also to our incredible crew; the lovely people who come along to the see the show recorded live and, of course, our wonderful contestants.

Nick Shearing is our greatest hero however. As well as being part of an incredible question writing team (more on them later) he has put in a huge amount of work into the book, as he also did last year. Thank you so much Nick! Thanks also to the wonderfully funny Moose Allain for the illustrations, and to our publishers Hodder & Stoughton for being so vague with the word 'deadline'.

Only 12 more letters to go. This is going better than I expected. Although I still have to do Q, X and Z . . .

Please enjoy this book responsibly, I don't want to hear of any cheating and resultant fist fights.

Questions are organised in groups of four, with answers

on the next page. This of course, leads to my worries about the cheating, the fist fights and the Boxing Day visits to A&E.

Remember this is the season of goodwill, especially when you find that Uncle Keith, who you foolishly left alone with the book, now has a suspiciously detailed knowledge of Peruvian lakes.

Sometimes people just know stuff about Peruvian lakes. Perhaps he's been there? Maybe during those 18 months in the 1990s when he was 'away' that no one in the family ever speaks about?

Though you're quite right, he probably has been cheating.

Uncle Keith is a liability, let's be honest.

Very near the end of the introduction now.

We hope you enjoy this book as much as we enjoyed writing it. It really has been a pleasure.

Xander and I would also like to thank you so much for watching *Pointless* and the lovely feedback you give us. It really is the best job in the television world. I would also like to personally thank Xander for having a name beginning with X, which has really got me out of a hole.

You'll find all sorts of facts in this book, and I promise they won't all be about Peruvian lakes. It's probably fitting to end this introduction with one of my favourite facts.

Zebra stripes are like fingerprints, no two are the same. Enjoy the book!

Angry angler Alan Allen arranges an array of anchovies
in an alcove under an ancient arch.

A – One of the five options whenever we have a picture round. The other four options are B, C, D and E. Always worth listening out for people saying 'we'll go with number A please', which happens surprisingly often.

Abi and Tracy – I love it when we have pairs of contestants whose names go together, such as Paul–Simon, and Moira–Stuart. I particularly liked it when contestants Abi and Tracy stood next to each other, and their name badges spelled out 'A bit racy'. This is nothing, however, compared to when our floor manager, Frosty, asked for a round of applause for two losing contestants called Tash and Gail and actually said, 'A round of applause for Gash and Tail'. That was the least of Frosty's many crimes, as anyone who has been to a recording will attest.

Acid Jazz – A category that hung around on our jackpot board for over a year and was never chosen, largely because no-one had a clue what it meant. Those clever backroom boffins changed it to 'Funky Music', where it was chosen by Beth and Andy. The question turned out to be 'Jamiroquai Top 40 Singles' and Beth and Andy gave us a pointless answer. I am almost certain there is a lesson for life there, though I have no idea what it is.

Alexander Armstrong – The shorter, better-educated of the two *Pointless* presenters, and really one of the loveliest men you could ever hope to meet. Armstrong lives in a heavily fortified castle in Oxfordshire with his four children and two wives. He is also an actor, a writer, a neurologist, a spy and a decathlete. He has many catchphrases (see **Great Contestants**).

Answers – (See **Questions**)

App – The *Pointless* app is available on phones, tablets and, as far as I know, landlines and via a series of hilltop beacons. I don't really understand how these things work, but apparently it is very addictive and if you download it, it will seriously affect your productivity for the next month or so.

Applause – When we started *Pointless* the audience would always applaud when the jackpot amount was revealed. When the jackpot was at its lowest possible point of £1,000, I sometimes felt that this applause was inappropriate. So now the audience only applauds when the jackpot is £2,000 or above. A little TV secret for you there.

Appleson – An entirely made-up word uttered by Bobby Ball, and probably the worst answer ever given on *Pointless Celebrities*. (For the full story see **Mack, Lee**)

Armadillo – A good answer, unless the question is, say, Women's Grand Slam Tennis Winners since 1970, in which case Petra Kvitová would be a better answer.

Azerbaijan – Always the best answer in any round about the Eurovision Song Contest. Also worth remembering that Morocco took part in 1980, the only African country ever to do so.

US STATES ENDING IN 'A'

We're looking for any state of the USA
whose name ends in the letter 'A'.

ALABAMA	53
ALASKA	40
ARIZONA	35
CALIFORNIA	62
FLORIDA	39
GEORGIA	12
INDIANA	9
IOWA	16
LOUISIANA	8
MINNESOTA	5
MONTANA	9
NEBRASKA	2
NEVADA	23
NORTH CAROLINA	12
NORTH DAKOTA	8
OKLAHOMA	15
PENNSYLVANIA	3
SOUTH CAROLINA	10
SOUTH DAKOTA	3
VIRGINIA	14
WEST VIRGINIA	5

ARTWORKS AND THEIR ARTISTS

We're going to show you the titles of twelve sculptures, or art installations, together with the year in which they were created. We are looking for the name of the artist who created each of them.

Angel Of The North (1997–1998)

Brillo Soap Pads Box (1964)

David (1501–1504)

The Discus Thrower (460 – 450 BC)

Little Dancer Aged Fourteen (1880 – 1881)

Lobster Telephone (1936)

Orbit (2012)

Mother And Child Divided (1993)

My Bed (1998)

Statue Of Liberty (1886)

Stringed Figure (Curlew), Version II (1956)

Walking Man (1947)

DOUBLE A-SIDES

We're going to show you the title of one song of a double A-side single that was a UK Top 40 hit, along with the artist who recorded it and the initials of the other song. We'd like you to give us the full title of the second song, please.

BONEY M – RIVERS OF BABYLON (BGITR)

BRUCE SPRINGSTEEN – BORN IN THE USA (IOF)

McFLY – ALL ABOUT YOU (YGAF)

QUEEN – BICYCLE RACE (FBG)

ROLLING STONES – RUBY TUESDAY (LSTNT)

ASTERIX BOOKS

We are looking for any of the English titles of the Asterix books written by Albert Uderzo and/or René Goscinny, and published by Orion prior to April 2011.

Bobby Billingham the bearded ballerina boldly battles
butterflies on the backs of a brace of burly bison.

Bangor Pier – This is the destination of our famous *Pointless* day trip. We get to see all sorts of lovely pictures in the head-to-head round, and when we've been in the studio at Elstree for weeks and weeks, the bright colours can sometimes go to our heads so that we coo over pictures of jellyfish and get a little bit giddy at pictures of sycamores. When a picture of Bangor Pier came up a couple of years ago, we just went NUTS over it and decided there and then that we had to plan a *Pointless* day trip to Bangor for us and all our viewers. We got it all planned, everything from who was doing the packed lunches (Dave and Moira from Galloway) to which of our favourite tunes we should sing on the way back ('Oh Danny Boy' and 'Price Tag'). It was going to be AMAZING. And then we just didn't get enough response from our viewers to make it worthwhile. Only 2,743,302 people said yes and, as Jan from Borehamwood Coaches pointed out, that would've meant there was going to be one mainly empty coach. If we'd got it up to 2,743,355 it would have been fine. Shame, it would have been a lovely day.

Before My Time – This started off being something that merely annoyed Richard; it has now become one of *Pointless*'s few grave transgressions (see **Red Card Offences**).

If a subject comes up – 80s music, 90s sitcoms, 70s sports stars – that pertains to a particular era that predates the birth of the contestant answering, it is now FORBIDDEN under the Osman Accord (2013) for that contestant to complain that the period was 'before my time'. Because if we all used that excuse then we wouldn't need to know anything about political history, the sketches of *That Was The Week That Was*, the carvings of Grinling Gibbons, or actors in *The Magnificent Seven* or *The Dirty Dozen*. And then where would we be? So let's hear no more of it.

Befriend – That's how you spell it. The 'i' before the 'e', just like in the rhyme. Simple when you see it in front of you like that and yet . . . and yet . . . It's one of those words I always have to write down before I *completely* trust it. Like 'field' (I *think* I've spelt that right – even as I look at it I realise that it too has the 'i' before the 'e'; it's almost like the people who came up with that rhyme were on to something). Anyway, it's the word I thought was going to be a pointless answer in the 'Words Ending In "IND"' round. It wasn't pointless as it turns out and I can still hear the decibels of laughter ringing in my ears sometimes at night. And then the kind voice of the primary school teacher who was a contestant on the show saying 'try and remember, Xander, that *Fri*-day comes at the *end* of the week.'

Actually, you people who came up with that rhyme, what about 'Either'? Eh? You're curiously quiet on that score.

Blue Peter – Over the years of doing *Pointless Celebrities* we have had so many *Blue Peter* presenters (collective noun: a biddy) that I have actually lost count. What I will say is that no-one is better schooled in *Pointless* information, and no-one better behaved under studio conditions, than the alumni of that flagship of the schedules (apart from Peter Purves, who was a right little imp from the moment he turned up: itching powder on Richard's chair and some extremely inappropriate graffiti left in his dressing room, daubed on the wall in who knows what).

Bow-dow-now-now-now – I love all *Pointless* recordings. Every single one. Looking out across the floor at the start of each show, seeing Frosty and Floor Paulie leading the applause (Floor Paulie shouting 'a-*pplause*' in that lovely way he has that makes it sound like he's shouting hooray); seeing Nigel our craneman (and sometime director) swinging his camera out over the audience; feeling the lighting state change for the opening piece; seeing the red light go on on my camera; hearing Nick (who's our director for this episode) in my ear saying 'Cue Xander!' and launching into the first segment of the show. And then massively cocking it up about a minute in so that we have to do it *all* over again; how could I possibly not? What, as they say, is not to love?

Well, nothing. But if there's one thing that makes it even better, that puts a big shiny cherry on top of the icing that is already *on* the cake, it's the sight of Frosty strutting about next to Camera 5 pretending he's got a huge bass guitar slung around his middle, plucking the invisible strings and singing 'bow-dow-now-now-now' along to the theme tune. Frosty, please never stop doing that.

Bread, That Ain't – For a short spell during *Pointless*'s third and fourth series, we pushed hard for a catchphrase. Obviously there are things that we each say a lot (see

Hiya, **Hello** and **Thank You Very Much Indeed**) but there was no question/response catchphrase along the lines of 'Nice to see you/To see you nice'. I suggested an ingenious device that Osman – though he may not remember it – had actually coined as a joke catchphrase when he and I were standing in the Endemol kitchenette (very close to an *actual* toaster) joshing about becoming game show hosts back in 2009. This was before one of the table reads of this zany new show we were trying out (when the BBC were still deciding if they even wanted to make *Pointless*). For a while it actually took off as a catchphrase, and if we could only remember to use it more often in the show it would embed and become an official *Pointless* 'thing' (it almost has done after a frankly derisory airing in a couple of episodes, so all it really needs is just a bit more effort on our part). The 'That ain't bread/ That's toast' formula also has the added benefit of actually *meaning* something and follows an internal logic all of its own. Can't say that for 'To see you nice' now can you?

Brown, James and Nick – Two of the luckiest guesses ever made on the show have been Brown answers. In the first case we were looking for any politician called David, Nick or Ed. The contestant, who confessed to knowing absolutely nothing about politics, closed her eyes and said

'Brown?' only to score a pointless answer (Nick Brown held various ministerial posts under Tony Blair and Gordon Brown.) In another category we were looking for the names of any actor in either *The Magnificent Seven* or *The Dirty Dozen*. The contestant, already holding up his hands in defeat, shook his head and said James Brown – which *I* obviously thought was hilarious and prompted any number of 'I wanna get up and do *my* thing' gags – only for it to score a pointless answer; an actor called Jim Brown played one of the smaller parts in the long, long cast list of *The Dirty Dozen* on IMDb. So there you are, if at a loss *always* go for a colour and an obvious first name. For example, Sam White, Sally Taupe and Bill Gentian would all be . . . well, they'd all be wrong and score a hundred points wouldn't they? But they would at least *sound* good.

Burghley House – This is in Cambridgeshire; the park of Burghley House is in Lincolnshire. The estate straddles the Lincs/Cambs border. That's official (from Burghley House itself). So to the question 'Which county is Burghley House in?' the correct answer is 'Cambridgeshire'.

WORDS BEGINNING AND ENDING IN 'B'

We are looking for any word that has its own entry in the *Oxford Dictionary of English* that begins and ends with the letter 'B'.

As usual we will not accept abbreviations, proper nouns, trademarks, or hyphenated words.

BACKCOMB	1	BLOB	20
BAFFLEGAB	0	BLUB	11
BAOBAB	2	BLURB	5
BARB	14	BOAB	0
BATHTUB	0	BOB	18
BEDAUB	0	BOMB	23
BEGOB	0	BOOB	15
BENUMB	0	BREADCRUMB	0
BIB	17	BREWPUB	0
BIBB	0	BUB	0
BICARB	0	BULB	11
BLAB	13	BURB	3
BLEB	1		

FAMOUS BARBARAS

Here is a list of clues which will
lead to a famous Barbara – can you tell
us who they are?

British sculptor died 1975

Famous for saying 'Walkies!'

Former MP married to author Ken

Had UK No.1 single with Elaine Paige

Her debut novel was *A Woman of Substance*

Hollywood star of *Double Indemnity*

Introduced breathalyser to UK

Mrs Ringo Starr's stage name

Prolific 'pink' British writer

Pseudonym of Ruth Rendell

US First Lady 1989 – 1993

Went from *Carry On* to *EastEnders*

BARBARA HEPWORTH	6
BARBARA WOODHOUSE	34
BARBARA FOLLETT	0
BARBARA DICKSON	16
BARBARA TAYLOR BRADFORD	17
BARBARA STANWYCK	9
BARBARA CASTLE	7
BARBARA BACH	19
BARBARA CARTLAND	42
BARBARA VINE	4
BARBARA BUSH	51
BARBARA WINDSOR	90

BATTLES

We're going to show you five anagrams of the names of famous battles (along with the century in which they took place). We want you to tell us the names of the battles.

N.B. The words 'Battle of' do not appear in the anagrams.

11TH CENTURY – STASHING

15TH CENTURY – OUT RACING

19TH CENTURY – TOOLWARE

20TH CENTURY – A TIN RIB

17TH CENTURY – DEMO GOERS

HASTINGS	48
AGINCOURT	15
WATERLOO	33
BRITAIN	35
SEDGEMOOR	0

BILL BRYSON BOOKS

We are looking for the title of any book written by Bill Bryson. We will accept collections, but will not accept *Icons of England*, which is a compilation edited, but not written, by Bryson. Nor will we accept *One Summer: America 1927*, which came out after this question was put to our 100 people.

Cantankerous cowboy Callum Crawford creeps across a crowded cafe in a Christmas cardigan.

Cake – A tradition which we have greatly encouraged is that of contestants bringing in cakes. Sometimes people bring us in biscuits, sometimes sweets, the occasional deluded contestant will bring something inedible (what are they thinking?). The sad truth, however, is that by the time the producers, researchers, and wardrobe and make-up artists have passed them around, Xander and I often don't get a look-in. Pauline from make-up and our producer John Ryan are the worst. I don't remember the last time I had a conversation with John where he didn't have crumbs around his mouth. My perfect cake would be a Lemon Drizzle, with 'Hands off Pauline and John' iced onto the top.

Central African Republic – The greatest pointless answer of all time. Ironically, it is no longer a pointless answer, simply because it is so famous for being so pointless. Probably the most extraordinary example of something becoming hugely famous for not being famous since the rise of Katie Hopkins.

Chase, The – Britain's second most popular teatime quiz. Third most popular if you count *Two Tribes*.

Cheating – The key rule in *Pointless* is that teams must not confer. I'm often asked if we've ever caught anyone cheating, and there are very much two answers to that question. The key thing you need to know is that the contestants are wearing microphones , and that Xander and I both wear earpieces that pick up every single word, and therefore we can answer the cheating question with some confidence. In over 800 episodes I have never once heard a contestant attempt to cheat.

Second, in over 100 episodes of *Pointless Celebrities*, there has never been any episode where someone hasn't tried to cheat. They simply can't help themselves, and Xander and I nervously have to tell them off, like newly qualified supply teachers. In fact the only celebrities I can categorically say have never cheated are the late, great Keith Harris, and Orville (see **Orville**). Those two are as good as gold. As a general rule, the celebrities do not shut up at any point, which means that, quite aside from their cheating, Xander and I pick up an awful lot of celebrity gossip. We could tell you things about Biggins that would make your hair curl.

Christmas Book – The three books it is compulsory to buy at Christmas are the annual Pointless Christmas book, the autobiography of a rugby player who has been on *Strictly Come Dancing* and a book about a brave cat. This is our fourth Christmas book and the other three are still widely available and we still make money if you buy them. If you already own the others then do make sure they haven't worn out and, if they have, think about buying replacement copies.

Chuckle Brothers – I'm often asked who would be my dream pairing on *Pointless Celebrities*. I frequently say 'Stephen Fry and Victoria Wood', or 'Daniel Radcliffe and Emma Watson', but in truth my dream pairing is the Chuckle Brothers. We've had them on three times now, and they are the loveliest gents you could hope to meet. Last time they were on I launched a campaign to get them knighted. At the time of publication, however, they are still not Sir Paul and Sir Barry Chuckle. Over to you, the Queen.

Computer – It is not on, it has never been on, except for one episode when we wondered what it would be like to turn it on. To discover the reasons it is there at all please cross-reference with our previous Christmas books, which, as previously mentioned, are still available (see **Christmas Book**).

COUNTRIES WHICH HAVE CAPITALS THAT START WITH THE SAME LETTER

We are looking for the name of any country with a capital city that has a name starting with the same letter as the first name of the country in English.

So, for example, France (which begins with 'F') would not count, as its capital city is Paris (which begins with a 'P'). We are using the normal 'short form' names for countries and we are excluding the word 'The' that may appear in the names of some countries.

And by 'country', we mean any sovereign state that is a member of the UN in its own right.

ALGERIA	5	MEXICO	15
ANDORRA	0	MONACO	1
BARBADOS	0	MOZAMBIQUE	0
BELGIUM	14	NIGER	0
BELIZE	1	PANAMA	3
BRAZIL	14	PAPUA NEW GUINEA	0
BRUNEI	0	SAN MARINO	0
BURUNDI	0	SÃO TOMÉ AND PRINCIPE	0
DJIBOUTI	0	SINGAPORE	3
GUATEMALA	1	SOUTH KOREA	2
GUYANA	0	SWEDEN	10
KUWAIT	1	TUNISIA	4
LUXEMBOURG	7	VANUATU	0
MALDIVES	0		
MARSHALL ISLANDS	0		

CHARACTERS AND THEIR CREATORS IN CHILDREN'S LITERATURE

We are going to show you twelve characters from children's books and we would like you tell us the name of the author who created them.

- **CARACTACUS POTT**
- **CRUELLA DE VIL**
- **DICKON SOWERBY**
- **FUNGUS THE BOGEYMAN**
- **JEMIMA PUDDLE-DUCK**
- **MATILDA WORMWOOD**
- **MR BUMP**
- **SHERE KHAN**
- **THE GRUFFALO**
- **TOM SAWYER**
- **TRACY BEAKER**
- **UGENIA LAVENDER**

IAN FLEMING	7
DODIE SMITH	4
FRANCES HODGSON BURNETT	0
RAYMOND BRIGGS	3
BEATRIX POTTER	33
ROALD DAHL	17
ROGER HARGREAVES	18
RUDYARD KIPLING	22
JULIA DONALDSON	6
MARK TWAIN	19
JACQUELINE WILSON	12
GERI HALLIWELL	0

POINTLESS FACT

In the film version of *Chitty-Chitty-Bang-Bang*, the name of the inventor was changed to Caractacus Potts.

CHRISTMAS HITS

We are about to show you the titles of five singles that were hits in the UK singles chart around Christmas time (along with the year in which they peaked) – but with the alternate letters missing. We'd like you to fill in the blanks and tell us the names of the songs.

C_R_S_M_S _N _M_R_L_N_ (1978)

K_L_I_G _N T_E _A_E (2009)

M_ B_O_B_ (1993)

M_R_Y _H_I_T_A_ E_E_Y_N_ (1985)

M_S_L_T_E _N_ W_N_ (1988)

STATIONS ON THE LONDON TUBE MAP BEGINNING WITH 'C'

We are looking for the full name of any station on the standard Transport for London Tube Map (issued in June 2012) that begins with the letter 'C'. This includes stations on the London Underground, London Overground railway line and the Docklands Light Railway.

CALEDONIAN ROAD	0
CALEDONIAN ROAD & BARNSBURY	0
CAMDEN ROAD	0
CAMDEN TOWN	8
CANADA WATER	3
CANARY WHARF	8
CANNING TOWN	9
CANNON STREET	8
CANONBURY	1
CANONS PARK	0
CARPENDERS PARK	0
CHALFONT & LATIMER	0
CHALK FARM	3
CHANCERY LANE	6
CHARING CROSS	43
CHESHAM	2
CHIGWELL	6

CHISWICK PARK	2
CHORLEYWOOD	3
CLAPHAM COMMON	1
CLAPHAM JUNCTION	1
CLAPHAM NORTH	0
CLAPHAM SOUTH	0
COCKFOSTERS	8
COLINDALE	3
COLLIERS WOOD	0
COVENT GARDEN	7
CROSSHARBOUR	1
CROUCH HILL	1
CROXLEY	0
CRYSTAL PALACE	0
CUSTOM HOUSE	0
CUTTY SARK	1
CYPRUS	0

Dauntless with derring-do, Davy Doyle the dustman
drives a delighted donkey down Dingly Dell in a
double decker dodgem.

Desk – When we first talked about how the show might look back in the kitchenette at Endemol in 2009 I was asked if I'd like to sit or stand. Richard had been given a desk, as he needed something for his never-switched-on laptop to sit on, and so he was being lined up for a chair (to this day I think a desk without a chair would have been plain odd, lending him a kind of 'I'm-just-going-to-finish-this-then-nip-out-for-a-snack' air, which would have made me feel hungry) but the feeling was that I should stand. I saw no reason to disagree with this, although these days when we are recording four shows a day I do revisit that conversation in my mind and wonder what sitting down might feel like. Mmmmmm. There is a particular concentric swirl of metallic board on Richard's desk at about shin height that catches everyone who walks past (Esther Rantzen) and even some people who walk past it daily (John Ryan, Frosty). It has never broken off yet but we only need Brian Blessed to come on a couple more times. . .

Double Dave – We occasionally get contestants who are called the same thing on the same show. You know when this has occurred because suddenly Steve from yesterday has come back as Steve H today. 'Ahh, and over there on podium 3 is the reason why: it's Steve G from Polzeath.' We have had several Daves on the show at the same time and on one occasion even on the same *team* on the same show. I know! Not one Dave in the team; but *two*. This phenomenon is known as Double Dave. We also once had two Marks on the show (see **Twain, Mark**)

Dressing Rooms – Richard and I each have one of these, thoughtfully situated in a corridor across from our studio (except for once when we were housed in a small trailer out on the Elstree lot – this arrangement lasted less than an hour on account of Richard's not being able to stand up to full height in his). They are havens of calm and quiet reflection except when *The Chase* is filming at Elstree, when they become redoubts into which we hurl ourselves from the No Man's Land of the corridor. They are also time machines, as we often leave the studio, go to our dressing rooms to change our suits and shirts, and when we come out it's another day. I still don't understand the quantum mechanics behind this.

DANIEL DAY-LEWIS FEATURE FILMS

We are looking for the title of any feature film that received a general cinema release for which Daniel Day-Lewis has an acting credit. We will not accept short films, TV films, documentaries or films in which he has played himself. We will accept voice performances.

We will not accept *My Beautiful Laundrette* as it was a TV film that later had a theatrical release. Nor will we accept *Sunday Bloody Sunday* (his debut film appearance, for which he was uncredited).

FAMOUS DOCTORS

The people on this list have all qualified as, or trained as, medical doctors. They may be famous in the field of medicine. Or they may be famous in an entirely different area.

Author of *A Study in Scarlet*

Author of *Jurassic Park*

Author of *The Motorcycle Diaries*

Father of antiseptic surgery

First man to run sub-four-minute mile

First successful human heart transplant

...Continued

FAMOUS DOCTORS

First woman to qualify as a doctor in the USA

Founder of Psychoanalysis

One of the 'Goodies'

Presenter of *Child of our Time*

Presenter of *TV Burp*

Writer of *Of Human Bondage*

ELIZABETH BLACKWELL	0
SIGMUND FREUD	39
GRAEME GARDEN	18
ROBERT WINSTON	21
HARRY HILL	82
WILLIAM SOMERSET MAUGHAM	0

DUBLIN

The following are all questions about people and places connected with Dublin, the capital city of Ireland. We would like you to tell us the answers.

Author of *Dracula* born here in 1847

Main stadium and HQ of the Gaelic Athletic Association

Man who founded a brewery in St James's Gate in 1759

Province in which Dublin is situated

The *Book of Kells* is housed in this university

DURAN DURAN UK TOP 40 SINGLES OF THE 1980s

We are looking for the title of any Duran Duran single which reached the Top 40 of the UK singles chart in the 1980s.

POINTLESS FACT

Our hunch is that one of our 100 had a lucky guess with 'Burning the Ground' – a somewhat obscure 'greatest-hits single' from 1989 made up of samples from earlier songs, whose title just happens to be a lyric from the chorus of Hungry Like the Wolf, but who are we to say.

Edward 'Exit' Ernst, an excitable escapologist, endures each episode of EastEnders ensconced under an end table.

Earth – When shown a very large, very clear picture of planet Earth, 89 of our 100 correctly identified it as 'Earth'. Or, to put it another way, 11 people didn't recognise it. Which means the Earth is recognised by about as many people as is David Hasselhoff. Please remember next time you're driving; those 11 people are out there somewhere.

Einsteinium – I am literally just about to get on to this in 'Elements' (see **Elements**). It's literally the next thing, so writing this is a waste of our time; it really shouldn't have its own entry at all. It's not like I'm short of things to put under 'E' or anything.

Elements – It has now been scientifically proven that young Brits currently learn more about the elements of the

Periodic Table from *Pointless* than they do from their Chemistry GCSE. An unusual side-effect of this is that the most famous elements in Britain are now Rutherfordium, Lawrencium and Einsteinium (don't bother seeing **Einsteinium**). So what actually are elements? We still have no idea.

Elstree Studios – In the same way that the Crucible Theatre is the home of World Snooker; Elstree Studios is the home of *Pointless*. No-one knows exactly where Elstree is, but you can get there by train so you don't actually need to know. We discovered recently that our studio – studio 8 – was used to film the Ewok scenes in *Return of the Jedi*. Elstree Studios is also the home of *Strictly Come Dancing*, *Room 101*, *Never Mind the Buzzcocks* and *Big Brother*. There is another, more secret part of Elstree Studios where *EastEnders* is filmed. Once, they let Xander and I walk around Albert Square, but we didn't see Ian Beale. We did see someone punching someone else in The Vic though, so it wasn't a wasted trip.

Eritrea – If you're looking for a new pointless country now that Central African Republic (see **Central African Republic**) is so famous, might I recommend Eritrea? It's next to Djibouti, and has lions and a thriving cement industry.

Equatorial Guinea – Probably even better than Eritrea (see **Eritrea**). Equatorial Guinea, the only officially Spanish-speaking country in Africa, has oil, so doesn't bother so much about having a cement industry. It is on the equator.

EUROVISION 'NUL POINTS' SCORERS

We are looking for any country that has finished with zero points at the end of a Grand Final of the Eurovision Song Contest, according to the official Eurovision website, from the 1957 contest up to the 2013 contest, inclusive. We are looking for the name of the country as it was at the time of their 'nul points' finish.

N.B. Although the first contest was held in 1956, the full results of that year's contest have never been made public, which is why our timeframe starts with the 1957 contest.

AUSTRIA	6
BELGIUM	8
FINLAND	19
GERMANY	13
ICELAND	14
ITALY	10
LITHUANIA	9
LUXEMBOURG	9
MONACO	2
NORWAY	39
PORTUGAL	10
SPAIN	21
SWEDEN	12
SWITZERLAND	10
THE NETHERLANDS	9
UNITED KINGDOM	58
TURKEY	13
YUGOSLAVIA	2

EASTENDERS CHARACTERS AND THEIR ACTORS

We will show you twelve names of *EastEnders* characters. We want to know the name of the actor who plays that character. Where a character has changed their name through marriage, we have supplied the surname by which they are best known.

ALFIE MOON

BIANCA JACKSON

DAVID WICKS

DOT COTTON

HEATHER TROTT

KAT SLATER

SHANE RICHIE	40
PATSY PALMER	23
MICHAEL FRENCH	4
JUNE BROWN	33
CHERYL FERGISON	4
JESSIE WALLACE	17

...Continued

EASTENDERS CHARACTERS AND THEIR ACTORS

KATHY BEALE

MO HARRIS

PAT BUTCHER

RAY DIXON

SHARON WATTS

TIFFANY MITCHELL

GILLIAN TAYLFORTH	21
LAILA MORSE	6
PAM ST. CLEMENT	26
CHUCKY VENN	0
LETITIA DEAN	19
MARTINE McCUTCHEON	13

EALING COMEDIES

We are about to show you the titles of five comedies produced by Ealing Studios, but with alternate letters missing. We'd like you to fill in the blanks and tell us the names of the films.

K_N_ H_A_T_ A_D _O_O_E_S

P_S_P_R_ T_ P_M_I_O

T_E _A_N_T

T_E _A_Y_I_L_R_

W_I_K_ G_L_R_!

EUROPEAN CAPITAL CITIES
SOUTH OF LONDON

We're looking for the capital city of any
country that is wholly or partly in Europe
and that is South of London.

By capital city, we mean the administrative
capital city of any sovereign state that
is a member of the UN.

ANDORRA LA VELLA	0
ANKARA	6
ASTANA	0
ATHENS	25
BAKU	0
BELGRADE	3
BERN	5
BRATISLAVA	1
BRUSSELS	8
BUCHAREST	5
BUDAPEST	5
CHISINĂU	0
KIEV	0
LISBON	25
LJUBLJANA	0
LUXEMBOURG	2
MADRID	41

MONACO	1
NICOSIA	0
PARIS	48
PODGORICA	0
PRAGUE	6
ROME	45
SAN MARINO	0
SARAJEVO	2
SKOPJE	2
SOFIA	4
TBILISI	0
TIRANA	3
VADUZ	0
VALLETTA	1
VIENNA	13
YEREVAN	0
ZAGREB	2

Fred the fly, in a feeding frenzy, flits back and forth
twixt a fox with a floppyfringe and a filthy fridge,
forcing food into his face.

Father Christmas – In our Christmas edition 2013 the ever wonderful Roy Wood was paired with the evergreen Father Christmas. Wood later complained that if Christmas hadn't shut up he would have 'twatted him one', which – for my money – makes me wonder if Roy really does wish it could be Christmas *every* day.

Faulks, Sebastian: The Works Of – In one head-to-head round this was the category that came up and neither of our pairs knew a SINGLE book by the wonderful Faulks (another person *Pointless* has a thing for, if we're honest). This prompted Richard to conjure up the scene back at Faulks Towers where Sebastian would have called his family down to watch his special round. I once went to a charity dinner that Faulks was hosting (brilliantly) and was banging on to my neighbour during his talk, so he stopped to wait for me to finish. I burn up with embarrassment every time I see or hear his name. Like now . . . aaaaaagghhh.

Family Fortunes – The devious uncle of *Pointless* that we don't really like to talk about.

Fancy Dress – The BBC keep trying to raise the production values of the Saturday 'Celebrity' edition of the show. Richard and I are forever being offered juggling elephants dancing on balls, or ladies in glittery swimming costumes and high heels and gentlemen in speedos with bow ties and cuffs (I've never quite understood that). We have so far rebuffed them but every so often we find that the wardrobe department has gone – quite literally – to town (Borehamwood isn't big on theatrical costumiers) and brought back shiny suits for 80s shows, Dickensian bits and bobs for Christmas shows (which always look great bobbing up and down on the sidelines as we stagily jiggle along from foot to foot to whichever Christmassy pop act is booked to play us out) or simply a sheepskin coat if it's a football-themed show (Richard lost just under two stone during the recording of that particular show – turns out sheepskin is really *warm*). We feel this is as much of a nod as we need to make to the razzmatazz of Saturday night. If you disagree then do please let us know.

Film – This is the subject everyone on *Pointless* says is one of their strong suits. Film, they'll say, and some kind of sport (Football, or Major League Baseball, or Rugby if they're Welsh or from the West Country). And yet when Film actually comes up as a category, usually in the guise of a specific auteur or actor (Hitchcock, for example, or Kurt Russell) they discover that enjoying going to the cinema is not the same thing as knowing about film. In final rounds the worst thing that can happen (see **Red Card Offences**) is that one of the pair decides that, despite his obsessive knowledge of MLB stats and teams since 1984, they shouldn't go for Baseball but should instead go for Film as it's something they can 'both have a go at'. So they end up inventing three Pedro Almodóvar titles (*The Cowboy, Spain in the Rain* and *The Cowboy Rides Again*) instead of dancing out of the studios with a £7,500 jackpot to spend on a trip to Australia for their niece's wedding.

Four Hundred Club – The Two Hundred Club is an august *Pointless* elite peopled by those teams that have managed to get both answers in a round wrong, usually thereby leaving the show with an unbeatably high total. Occasionally we have two teams tied on 200, which triggers the exciting state of Lockdown (see **Lockdown, Monks Of**). If a team succeeds in scoring two hundred in two rounds that team then joins the Four Hundred Club. If they manage it by going out in the first round on each occasion with 200 on their podium scoreboard, then they get exclusive Golden Four Hundred Club membership, which entitles them to wear the distinctive matching brown tie and pocket-kerchief (which to date no-one has bought from the club shop).

In one round in 2012, the category was Robert Redford Films and only three (3) of the eight players had actually heard of Robert Redford (see **Film** above). This resulted in wrong answers from each of the four contestants going up the line (including – brilliantly – *Seven Samurai* and *Prince of Persia*) and two wrong answers coming back down, and then another wrong answer in the subsequent Lockdown tie-break. This was on a day when Fulham were playing at home and Richard was meant to be slipping into his debenture at Craven Cottage just as soon as he could get there after we'd finished. We were barely into the head-to-head when the final whistle blew. Technical or General Knowledge breakdowns invariably follow a pattern that is suspiciously close to FFC's home fixture list.

F1 WORLD CHAMPIONS

We are about to show you a list of six nationalities on the board. We would like you to name any man who is one of these nationalities to have won the F1 World Drivers' championship, from its inception in 1950, up to and including the 2012 title.

For the avoidance of doubt, we are taking the nationalities of the drivers from the official F1 website.

The nationalities are:

- BRITISH
- GERMAN
- BRAZILIAN
- ITALIAN
- FINNISH
- AUSTRALIAN

AUSTRALIAN

| ALAN JONES | 4 |
| JACK BRABHAM | 8 |

BRAZILIAN

AYRTON SENNA	44
EMERSON FITTIPALDI	10
NELSON PIQUET	6

BRITISH

DAMON HILL	38
GRAHAM HILL	16
JACKIE STEWART	1
JAMES HUNT	7
JENSON BUTTON	41
JIM CLARK	2

JOHN SURTEES	2
LEWIS HAMILTON	48
MIKE HAWTHORN	0
NIGEL MANSELL	25

FINNISH

KEKE ROSBERG	2
KIMI RÄIKKÖNEN	9
MIKA HÄKKINEN	23

GERMAN

| MICHAEL SCHUMACHER | 71 |
| SEBASTIAN VETTEL | 22 |

ITALIAN

| NINO FARINA | 1 |
| ALBERTO ASCARI | 2 |

FEMALE FIRSTS

We're going to show you twelve 'firsts' concerning women. We want you to name the women who were first to achieve the feats listed.

Appear on a postage stamp

Be Head of MI5

Cox in the University Boat Race

Go into space

Marry Henry VIII

Run for US Vice-President as Republican

Sit in House of Commons for Green Party

The First Test Tube Baby

Train a Grand National winner

Win a Best Director Oscar

Win a Nobel Prize

Win Eurovision for the UK

QUEEN VICTORIA	38
STELLA RIMINGTON	3
SUE BROWN	0
VALENTINA TERESHKOVA	1
CATHERINE OF ARAGON	20
SARAH PALIN	14
CAROLINE LUCAS	1
LOUISE BROWN	8
JENNY PITMAN	12
KATHRYN BIGELOW	2
MARIE CURIE	17
SANDIE SHAW	16

UK FORESTS

We're going to show you the names of five forests located in the United Kingdom, but with alternate letters removed. We'd like you to fill in the blanks and name the forest you think the fewest of our 100 knew.

E_P_N_ F_R_S_

F_R_S_ O_ D_A_

G_Y_Y_ F_R_S_

S_E_W_O_ F_R_S_

S_V_R_A_E _O_E_T

EPPING FOREST	48
FOREST OF DEAN	39
GWYDYR FOREST	0
SHERWOOD FOREST	56
SAVERNAKE FOREST	6

FAMOUS FIVE NOVELS

We are looking for the titles of Enid Blyton's *Famous Five* novels. All begin with 'Five. . .'

We are only looking for the titles of full-length novels originally published between 1942 and 1963.

Glenda Gillham, a go-getting grandmother, glamorises her goat with gifts of gloves and Gaultier galoshes.

Geoff – One of the absolute classic *Pointless* contestant names. Keen viewers will remember our infamous 'surfeit of Geoffs', which saw five Geoffs compete within a week. Crazy days. Perhaps they should think about putting up a blue plaque?

Germany – We very rarely accept United Kingdom as an answer to questions about Europe, and so Germany almost always tops the polls. I make no comment about this, as both world wars were a long time ago, and all is very much forgiven. Although Fulham fans haven't quite forgiven Germany for sending us Felix Magath yet. Germany was also included in a round involving anagrams of European countries, where we discovered that it is, rather neatly, an anagram of 'Meg Ryan'.

Glamour – I was once asked if recording *Pointless* was 'as glamorous as it looks', and I have to say that, yes, it is pretty much exactly as glamorous as it looks. For example, a pigeon once flew into the studio. Perhaps another blue plaque is called for.

Gosport – A town which we once had some contestants from. As far as I remember it is in Hampshire, but don't quote me on that. Other contestants on the show have been from Redditch, Oswestry, St Austell and other places.

Grandparents – We have all sorts of combinations pairing up on *Pointless*: parents with kids, partners, workmates, 'friends' who we secretly think are having an affair, fathers-in-law desperately attempting to bond with inappropriate sons-in-law, and so on. But our favourite pairings are always Grandparent with Grandchild. Is there a happier, more charming relationship in existence? They always lose, mind you. That's the circle of life for you.

Great Contestants – So why does Xander always say that people have been 'great contestants' even when they have said that William Tell wrote *Hamlet* (see **William Tell**)? The truth is that he is a really nice man, that appearing on *Pointless* is quite stressful, and that being nice to each other is the only true secret to making the world a happier place.

Green Room – The 'Green Room' is the place where TV shows traditionally hold their pre- and post-show hospitality. Our 'Green Room' is actually a 'Magnolia Room That Could Do With A Lick Of Paint And Some More Cushions' and is exclusively for the contestants. We often get asked what goes on in the *Pointless* Green Room but the truth is that Xander and I wouldn't know. What the contestants get up to in the Green Room is very much their business. Certainly a lot of them appear to be drunk by the time filming begins, but, to be honest, that tends to make them easier to control.

ENGLAND GOALKEEPERS

We are looking for the name of anyone who has played in goal for the England national football team, from 1966 through to the start of 2011 inclusive. Players will only count if they have actually played in goal – unused substitutes will not count.

We will not accept Jack Butland, John Ruddy or Fraser Forster, as they all played their first games for England after this time period.

ALEX STEPNEY	2	JOE HART	16
BEN FOSTER	8	NIGEL MARTYN	4
CHRIS KIRKLAND	3	NIGEL SPINK	0
CHRIS WOODS	7	PAUL ROBINSON	14
DAVE BEASANT	1	PETER BONETTI	8
DAVID JAMES	35	PETER SHILTON	53
DAVID SEAMAN	55	PHIL PARKES	2
GARY BAILEY	1	RAY CLEMENCE	17
GORDON BANKS	28	RICHARD WRIGHT	0
GORDON WEST	1	ROBERT GREEN	25
IAN WALKER	1	RON SPRINGETT	1
JIMMY RIMMER	0	SCOTT CARSON	7
JOE CORRIGAN	1	TIM FLOWERS	4

GAME SHOWS

We are going to show you twelve descriptions of UK game shows. We would like you to name the show from the clue.

Based on the American game show, *Family Feud*

Contestant Charles Ingram was found guilty of cheating on this show in 2001

Dale Winton invited contestants to go *Wild in the Aisles*

Earned Anne Robinson her crown as 'The Queen of Mean'

Players could choose between a 'physical', a 'mental', a 'skill' or a 'mystery' game

Presented by Ant & Dec, this show made the contestants choose between two colours

GAME SHOWS

Show in which five quizzers take on five of the UK's finest quiz brains

Simon Cowell appeared as a contestant on this show in 1990

The final part of the show was to memorise items on a conveyer belt

The show which gave hostess Carol Smillie her break into TV

This show's consolation prize was a silver cheque book and pen

Victoria Coren's highbrow puzzle game on BBC Four

GREEN FOOD

Here are five anagrams of the names of foods that are commonly green. We'd like you to work out what they are and give us the most obscure.

APE

CRUMB CUE

ERECT GOUT

TAUT GNOME

WIKI IF RUT

PEA	92
CUCUMBER	72
COURGETTE	7
MANGE TOUT	22
KIWIFRUIT	12

THE GRAND NATIONAL

JOCKEY

We are looking for the name of any jockey who has ridden the winner in an Aintree Grand National on at least two occasions in races held since 1945 up to and including the 2012 Grand National.

TRAINER

We are looking for the name of any trainer of a horse that has won the Aintree Grand National since 1945 up to and including the 2012 Grand National.

HORSE

We are looking for any horse with a one-word name who has won the Aintree Grand National since 1945 up to and including the 2012 race.

For the purposes of the question, we are not accepting either E.S.B or L'Escargot as one-word names, even though they both are names of horses that have won the Grand National.

JOCKEY

ARTHUR THOMPSON	0
BRIAN FLETCHER	0
BRYAN MARSHALL	0
CARL LLEWELLYN	0
FRED WINTER	0
PAT TAAFFE	0
RICHARD DUNWOODY	1
RUBY WALSH	2

TRAINER

ANDREW TURNELL	0
BOBBY RENTON	0
DAN MOORE	0
DAVID BARONS	0
DAVID ELSWORTH	0
DAVID PIPE	1
DENYS SMITH	0
DONALD McCAIN, JR	0
FRANK GILMAN	0
FRANK HUDSON	0

FRED RIMELL	0
FRED WINTER	0
FULKE WALWYN	0
GEORGE OWEN	0
GINGER McCAIN	2
GORDON ELLIOTT	0
GORDON W. RICHARDS	0
HERBERT McDOWELL	0
JACK O'DONOGHUE	0
JENNY PITMAN	7
JIMMY MANGAN	0
JOHN KEMPTON	0
JOHN LEADBETTER	0
JOHN SUTCLIFFE	0
JONJO O'NEILL	1
JOSH GIFFORD	1
KEITH PIGGOTT	0
KIM BAILEY	0
MARTIN BRASSIL	0
MARTIN PIPE	0
MICHAEL OLIVER	0

NEVILLE CRUMP	0	AYALA	0
NICK GASELEE	0	BALLABRIGGS	4
NIGEL TWISTON-DAVIES	0	BINDAREE	0
NORMAN MASON	0	BOBBYJO	0
PAUL NICHOLLS	1	CAUGHOO	0
RYAN PRICE	0	CORBIERE	1
STEVE BROOKSHAW	0	FOINAVON	2
TED WALSH	2	FREEBOOTER	0
TERRY CASEY	0	GRITTAR	0
TIM FORSTER	0	HEDGEHUNTER	1
TOBY BALDING	1	KILMORE	0
TOM TAAFFE, SR	0	LUCIUS	0
TOMMY CARBERRY	0	MIINNEHOMA	0
TOMMY RAYSON	0	NUMBERSIXVALVERDE	0
VENETIA WILLIAMS	0	OXO	0
VINCENT O'BRIEN	0	PAPILLON	1
WILLIE MULLINS	0	RUBSTIC	0
WILLIE STEPHENSON	0	SEAGRAM	1
		SPECIFY	0

HORSE

		SUNDEW	0
ALDANITI	9	TEAL	0
ANGLO	0		

Henry Hurst, a hirsute hipster in a Homburg,
hides a handful of humbugs in the hammock of
homesick hermit Herman Hill.

Hambleton – A village in Lancashire which has been home to a couple of *Pointless* contestants but which – disappointingly – is *not* where *Playschool*'s toy, Hamble, came from.

Hiya, Hello – This is most people's favourite of Richard's catchphrases. It happens every single show after my rambling introduction, and always follows the words '. . . it's my pointless friend Richard.' The 'Hiya' element is down the camera to the audience at home and the 'Hello' to the studio audience. Richard would of course prefer to say 'Good Afternoon' or 'Good Evening' but we never know what time of year a show might go out. In the summer 5.15pm is definitely afternoon, but in the winter it's practically the middle of the night.

Humble Pie – Occasionally I offer to eat my podium in the event of something unlikely happening on the show. It is the almost inevitable precursor to that thing then happening. To date I have not eaten my podium – the intricate electronics would be expensive to replace and I'd probably have to pay for them.

HITCHCOCK FILMS IN COLOUR

We are looking for the title of any feature film directed by Alfred Hitchcock which was filmed entirely in colour. Short films, documentaries and films in which Hitchcock was uncredited do not count.

HARRYS AND HENRYS

We are going to show you fourteen descriptions of famous people who all are known by the first name 'Harry' or 'Henry'. We would like you to give us their surnames. As ever, you are looking for the answer the fewest of our 100 people knew.

18th-century English chemist who identified hydrogen (1731–1810)

Boxing commentator who often interviewed Frank Bruno post-fight (1925–2010)

English comedian who created the character 'Loadsamoney' (b.1961)

Former manager of Portsmouth and Southampton football clubs (b.1947)

Presenter of TV shows *Game for a Laugh* and *Going for Gold* (b.1946)

Stage name of the escapologist Erik Weisz (1874–1926)

Star of the original *Clash of the Titans* film (b.1951)

HARRYS AND HENRYS

The first boxer to receive a knighthood (1934–2011)

UK Liberal Prime Minister (1836–1908)

US car manufacturer who introduced assembly line production for his Model T (1863–1947)

US composer who wrote 'Moon River' and the 'Pink Panther' theme (1924–1994)

US novelist who wrote *The Turn of the Screw* (1843–1916)

US President at the end of WWII (1884–1972)

US Secretary of State who won the 1973 Nobel Peace Prize (b.1923)

THE HITCHHIKER'S GUIDE TO THE GALAXY

We are going to show you five clues to facts about the science fiction comedy series known as *The Hitchhiker's Guide to the Galaxy*. We would like you to give us the answer to the clue you think the fewest of our 100 people knew.

Alien race, known for their awful poetry, who destroy the Earth

Created by this British writer

Name of the guitarist in the rock band Disaster Area that features in the series

Number that is the answer to 'Life, The Universe, and Everything'

Two words printed on the Guide 'in large friendly letters'

TEAMS MANAGED BY ROY HODGSON

We are looking for the name of any professional club or international team managed by Roy Hodgson prior to his appointment as England manager in May 2012.

BLACKBURN ROVERS	9
BRISTOL CITY	2
FC COPENHAGEN	0
FINLAND	6
FULHAM	31
HALMSTAD	1
INTERNAZIONALE (INTER MILAN)	13
LIVERPOOL	46
MALMÖ FF	3
NEUCHÂTEL XAMAX	0
ODDEVOLD	0
OREBRO	0
SWITZERLAND	19
UDINESE	1
UNITED ARAB EMIRATES	2
VIKING	1
WEST BROMWICH ALBION	39
GRASSHOPPER (ZÜRICH)	0

Out in the inhospitable icefields on an igneous island,
the ignominious Doctor Ignatius Inksmith inveigles
igloos from indigenous Inuit.

Illness – Every now and again you come into work even though you have a cold, because you are terrifically brave. You sit at your desk drinking Lemsip, waving away offers of help like the hero you are. Then, the next day, or the day after, your cold disappears and it's someone else's turn to slack off and get all the attention. The problem with filming *Pointless*, however, is that, because we film four episodes a day, if you turn up with a cold then it lasts all week on television. Two days' illness essentially lasts for two weeks in TV terms, and leads to all sorts of concerned tweets worrying about your long-term health. Equally, if you ever have a bad haircut, while yours might grow out in a couple of weeks, mine and Xander's last for six months, and are then repeatedly endlessly on Challenge.

Inca – Probably my favourite episode ever was a *Blue Peter* special of *Pointless Celebrities*. This was not only because I got to meet Tim Vincent, but also because throughout the show I had a dog sleeping by my desk. That dog was Inca, a beautiful and impeccably behaved Border Collie. I tried to keep her forever, but no luck. I also had a tortoise on my desk in that show, but he was less fun. No offence to tortoises.

Incorrect Answers – There have been some classic incorrect answers on *Pointless* (see **Appleson**, **JFK** and **William Tell**) but other contestants have been much more unlucky. Sometimes when an answer is 'slightly' wrong we give it, and sometimes we don't. That decision is never taken by me, but by the producers and question writers. They always have to think of fairness to the contestant involved, but also to the other contestants. One principle is that if you get something very *complicated* slightly wrong we'll probably give you the benefit of the doubt, but if you get something *obvious* slightly wrong then it's not fair to the others to accept it. So if you answer 'Cliff Richards' instead of 'Cliff Richard' it wouldn't be allowed, but if you said the President of Argentina was 'Christine Fernandez de Kirchner' instead of 'Christina Fernandez de Kirchner' then we'd accept it.

It's an inexact science, but we try to be as fair as possible.

International Versions – *Pointless* is made in lots of countries around the world, including France, Germany and, most excitingly, Macedonia. Some countries, including France I'm afraid, seem to think that *Pointless* can be made without having a spectacle-wearing sidekick sitting in front of a pretend computer. That sounds terrible! The pun 'Pointless' doesn't work anywhere else, so the Croatian version is called 'No-one Thought of That' (or whatever that is in Croatian), the Polish version is 'Only You' and the Swiss call it 'Less is More'. An American version of the show is due to begin in 2016. I don't yet know what that's going to be called, but my guess would be 'Hey Buddy, Ain't No-one Never Said That Answer, No Sir!'

Ipswich Town – Our football questions can add fire to many local rivalries, as fans can see at a glance which teams are the most famous. For the record, Manchester United always score more than Manchester City, Southampton beat Portsmouth, Liverpool beat Everton, Arsenal beat Spurs, and, usually the closest of all, Ipswich Town edge out Norwich City.

Irish People – It is a great sadness that although lots of people in the Republic of Ireland watch *Pointless*, they are not allowed to be contestants. This is because, for reasons to do with prize money, only Licence Fee payers are eligible. Other countries beginning with 'I' that are also banned from appearing are Italy, India, Israel, Indonesia, Iran and Iraq. Though we get fewer complaints about it from any of them. Incidentally, can you name the only country in the world beginning with 'I' that I have left out of that list?

It Was Iceland – You know, that other country beginning with 'I'.

ELEMENTS WITH NAMES THAT DO NOT CONTAIN THE LETTER 'I'

We are looking for any chemical element from the periodic table whose name does not contain the letter 'I'.

ARGON	11
BORON	6
CARBON	15
COBALT	2
COPPER	16
GOLD	25
HYDROGEN	25
KRYPTON	6
LANTHANUM	0
LEAD	13
MANGANESE	4
MERCURY	10
MOLYBDENUM	1
NEON	11
OXYGEN	23
PHOSPHORUS	3
RADON	4
SULPHUR	6
TANTALUM	0
TUNGSTEN	2
XENON	7

FAMOUS ITALIANS

The following is a list of clues to famous people who were born in Italy or what now makes up modern Italy. We want you to tell us who they are. We will accept either their surname or the name by which they are commonly known.

Chef who won the 2009 *I'm A Celebrity . . .*

Composed the opera 'La Boheme'

Constructed an electric battery c.1800

Diminutive Chelsea number 25 (1996–2003)

Directed the 1960 film *La Dolce Vita*

Fashion designer born in Piacenza in 1934

FAMOUS ITALIANS

Italy's longest serving post-war PM

Jockey won seven races in one day at Ascot in 1996

One of the original 'Three Tenors'

Painted the ceiling of the Sistine Chapel

Starred opposite Cary Grant in *Houseboat*

Wrote *Accidental Death of an Anarchist*

SILVIO BERLUSCONI	14
FRANKIE DETTORI	34
LUCIANO PAVAROTTI	39
MICHELANGELO	34
SOPHIA LOREN	14
DARIO FO	0

COUNTRIES THAT BORDER INDIA

We are looking for the name of any country that shares a land border with India. By 'country', we mean any sovereign state that is a member of the UN in its own right.

BANGLADESH	48
BHUTAN	17
BURMA	13
CHINA	47
NEPAL	46
PAKISTAN	88

ACTORS IN THE *INDIANA JONES* FILM SERIES

We are looking for any actor who received an acting credit according to IMDb in any of the four Indiana Jones films. That is *Raiders of the Lost Ark, The Temple of Doom, The Last Crusade* and *The Kingdom of the Crystal Skull*.

We will not accept Michael Sheard (a.k.a. Grange Hill's Mr Bronson) as his role as Hitler in *Indiana Jones and the Last Crusade* was uncredited.

AHMED EL SHENAWI	0	CAROL BEBBINGTON	0
AKIO MITAMURA	0	CATE BLANCHETT	0
ALAN DALE	0	CHET HANKS	0
ALEX HYDE-WHITE	0	CHRIS JENKINSON	0
ALEXEI SAYLE	0	CHRIS FREDERICK	0
ALFRED MOLINA	0	CHRISTINE CARTWRIGHT	0
ALISON DOODY	0	CHRISTOPHER TODD	0
AMRISH PURI	0	CHUA KAH JOO	0
ANDREA CHANCE	0	CLARE SMALLEY	0
ANDREW DIVOFF	0	CORINNE BARTON	0
ANTHONY CHINN	0	D.M. DENAWAKE	0
ANTHONY HIGGINS	0	D.R. NANAYAKKARA	0
ARJUN PANDHER	0	DAN AYKROYD	0
ART REPOLA	0	DAVID MURRAY	0
AUDI RESENDEZ	0	DAVID YIP	1
BHASKER PATEL	0	DAWN REDDALL	0
BILL REIMBOLD	0	DEAN GRIMES	0
BILLY J. MITCHELL	0	DEBBIE ASTELL	0
BRADLEY GREGG	0	DEIRDRE LAIRD	0
BRENDA GLASSMAN	0	DENHOLM ELLIOTT	1
BRIAN KNUTSON	0	DENNIS NUSBAUM	0
CARLOS LINARES	0	DHARMADASA KURUPPU	0

DHARSHANA PANANGALA	0	ILIA VOLOK	0
DIMITRI DIATCHENKO	0	IRANGANIE SERASINGHE	0
DON FELLOWS	0	ISHAQ BUX	0
EDDIE TAGOE	0	ISLA BLAIR	0
ELAINE GOUGH	0	J.J. HARDY	0
ELIZABETH BURVILLE	0	JAN COLTON	0
EMMANUEL TODOROV	0	JEFF O'HACO	0
ERNIE REYES JR.	0	JENNY TURNOCK	0
EUGENE LIPINSKI	0	JERRY HARTE	0
FRANK MARSHALL	0	JIM BROADBENT	0
FRANK OLEGARIO	0	JOEL STOFFER	0
FRED SORENSON	0	JOHN HURT	2
FREDERICK JAEGER	0	JOHN REES	0
GAYNOR MARTINE	0	JOHN RHYS-DAVIES	1
GEORGE HARRIS	0	JON VALERA	0
GEORGE MALPAS	0	JULIA MARSTAND	0
GRAEME CROWTHER	0	JULIAN GLOVER	0
GUSTAVO HERNANDEZ	0	JULIE ECCLES	0
HARRISON FORD	36	JULIE KIRK	0
HELENA BARRETT	0	KAREN ALLEN	0
IGOR JIJIKINE	0	KATE CAPSHAW	2

KE HUY QUAN	0	MOTI MAKAN	0
KEVIN COLLINS	0	NEIL FLYNN	0
KEVORK MALIKYAN	0	NICOLA SCOTT	0
KIRAN SHAH	0	NICOLE LUTHER	0
LARRY SANDERS	0	NINA ARMSTRONG	0
LEE SPRINTALL	0	NINA MCMAHON	0
LISA MULIDORE	0	NITO LARIOZA	0
LORRAINE DOYLE	0	NIZWAR KARANJ	0
LOUIS SHELDON	0	PASHA D. LYCHNIKOFF	0
LOUISE DALGLEISH	0	PAT ROACH	0
LUKE HANSON	0	PATRICK DURKIN	0
MALCOLM WEAVER	0	PAUL FREEMAN	1
MARC MILES	0	PAUL HUMPOLETZ	0
MARIA LUISA MINELLI	0	PAUL MAXWELL	0
MARISA CAMPBELL	0	PETER PACEY	0
MARTIN GORDON	0	PHILIP STONE	0
MARTIN KREIDT	0	PHILIP TAN	0
MATTHEW SCURFIELD	0	RAJ SINGH	0
MAUREEN BACCHUS	0	RAY WINSTONE	1
MELLAN MITCHELL	0	REBEKKAH SEKYI	0
MICHAEL BYRNE	0	REX NGUI	0
MICHAEL YAMA	0	RIC YOUNG	0

RICHARD YOUNG	0		SUE HADLEIGH	0
RIVER PHOENIX	1		SUZANNE ROQUETTE	0
ROBERT BAKER	0		T. RYAN MOONEY	0
ROBERT EDDISON	0		TED GROSSMAN	0
RONALD LACEY	0		TERRY RICHARDS	0
ROY CHIAO	0		TIM HISER	0
RUBY DE MEL	0		TOM BRANCH	0
ROSHAN SETH	0		TONY VOGEL	0
RUTH WELBY	0		TUTTE LEMKOW	0
SAMANTHA HUGHES	0		V.J. FOSTER	0
SARAH-JANE HASSELL	0		VANESSA FIELDWRIGHT	0
SASHA SPIELBERG	0		VENIAMIN MANZYUK	0
SEAN CONNERY	24		VERNON DOBTCHEFF	0
SHARON BOONE	0		VIC TABLIAN	0
SHIA LABEOUF	6		VICKI MCDONALD	0
SONNY CALDINEZ	0		VINCE DEADRICK SR.	0
SOPHIA STEWART	0		WILL MILES	0
SOUAD MESSAOUDI	0		WILLIAM HOOTKINS	0
STANY DE SILVA	0		WOLF KAHLER	0
STEFAN KALIPHA	0		ZIA GELANI	0
STEVE HANSON	0			

In jumpers, jodhpurs, and jerkins, Jack and Jill jive and jitterbug into a jacuzzi full of jolly jellyfish.

Jackpot – When we first started making the show there were one or two comments made about the modest jackpot. This, you have to remember, was in the days of *The Weakest Link* and *Who Wants to be a Millionaire?* in which a contestant (if they were only clever enough) could walk away with enough to buy a holiday in Barbados or, on a really good day, pay off a mortgage. The average *Pointless* jackpot will buy you a couple of return tickets to Alnmouth, a night at the White Swan in Alnwick and entry for two to Alnwick Castle gardens for a day (what am I, a travel agent?). And as time's gone by, everyone's just got used to the smaller sums involved.

But it doesn't take much for it to get exciting, sometimes very exciting indeed. If only a handful of consecutive couples go for Film instead of Major League Baseball in the final round and the jackpot is allowed to build for a few days to, say, £5,000 and beyond, then it turns into a Meaningful Sum Of Money. Suddenly there's a new atmosphere on the studio floor and the affable retired civil servant of yesterday has come back with a steely edge and you wonder just how much of the return train journey to Runcorn will be spent in silence if Sally, his wife of thirty-nine years, can't remember a female tennis player with four or more grand slam titles to her name. It used to be said that I would only ask contestants what they would do with the jackpot if they were indeed about to win it, but that would have taken levels of competence way beyond my simple grasp, and, anyway, I don't know what the result is until the column drops so it must have been coincidental. I now make a point of asking it every show before the first question gets columned, just to make it the same for everyone.

Oh, and by the way, Sally's just come up with Margaret Court and got a pointless answer. Wa-hey!

Jedward –The Irish twins came on *Pointless Celebrities* in 2015, wore their hair down (or possibly had been caught in a Borehamwood downpour without their rainhoods) and were absolutely fine. John even gave me his tie. They called me Al the whole way through the recording which, although I'm no Paul Simon, I still found rather charming. For the few days surrounding their appearance on the show, Richard and I were included in all their Twitter correspondence and the love those two inspire among their followers made me look briefly at the world – and indeed Jedward – through new eyes.

JFK – My favourite wrong answer of all time. The round was a Historical Figures round and one of the boarded clues said 'Assassinated by Lee Harvey Oswald in Dallas'. Gemma, who was answering, had absolutely no hesitation in saying 'JR'.

Jizz – Back in the long, long ago, when we were making our first ever series of *Pointless*, we were still new to the whole teatime family show thing and hadn't yet learnt to prohibit certain words from broadcast. So when the category Words Ending In 'ZZ' came up and Michael – a very sweet-natured student (who even forewarned us that his answer was 'profane') – came up with 'jizz', we were obliged to keep a straight face and treat it like a perfectly normal answer. As Richard explained at the time, 'jizz' means the first impression you get of a plant or animal and it scored an admirably low 7. But we all knew that. These days, rude words and shamed stars of the 70s are gently removed from potential answer lists to avoid anyone being put off their fish fingers.

Jobs – When we meet our contestants at the beginning of each show, I ask them what they do. This is more because it's a relatively easy way of getting a conversation started than because I am compiling a dossier on What People Do (although I am obviously doing that too – based on the data gathered from *Pointless* there are very few piano tuners and hod-carriers out there). Some jobs open up all sorts of conversational vistas ('And what do you do, Morag?' 'I train dolphins to rescue stricken vessels.') and some less so ('And what keeps you busy in Whitchurch, Mike?' 'I'm a civil servant.' 'Can I ask what branch of the civil service you're in?' 'No.'). You can tell how highly I rate the chattability of a job by the speed with which I then ask, 'And what are your hobbies?' ('What do you do, Simon?' 'I work in IT for a legal—' 'And what are your hobbies?')

Jumpers – Richard and I have received several scarves to date, even knitted dolls of ourselves, but up to this point no jumpers. This is quite possibly a good thing.

JACKSON UK TOP 40 SINGLES

We are looking for any song released by Michael Jackson, the Jackson 5 or The Jacksons which reached the Top 40 of the UK singles chart up to the end of January 2013. We will accept a title only once. We will not accept remixes or EPs. Double A-sides will be accepted as separate answers.

ABC	19	DON'T STOP 'TIL YOU GET ENOUGH	3
AIN'T NO SUNSHINE	1	DREAMER	0
ANOTHER PART OF ME	0	EARTH SONG	15
BAD	31	EVEN THOUGH YOU'RE GONE	0
BEAT IT	18	FAREWELL MY SUMMER LOVE	0
BEN	27		
BILLIE JEAN	43	GET IT	0
BLACK OR WHITE	20	GHOSTS	0
BLAME IT ON THE BOOGIE	13	GIRL YOU'RE SO TOGETHER	0
BLOOD ON THE DANCE FLOOR	1	GIVE IN TO ME	0
		GOIN' PLACES	0
CAN YOU FEEL IT	2	GONE TOO SOON	0
COME TOGETHER	0	GOT TO BE THERE	5
CRY	0	HALLELUJAH DAY	0
DESTINY	0	HEAL THE WORLD	3
DIRTY DIANA	10	HISTORY	2
DOCTOR MY EYES	0		

HOLD MY HAND	0	ONE DAY IN YOUR LIFE	2
I JUST CAN'T STOP LOVING YOU	0	ONE MORE CHANCE	0
I WANT YOU BACK	6	P.Y.T. (PRETTY YOUNG THING)	0
I'LL BE THERE	0	REMEMBER THE TIME	0
IN THE CLOSET	0	ROCK WITH YOU	5
JAM	0	ROCKIN' ROBIN	11
LEAVE ME ALONE	1	SAY SAY SAY	2
LIBERIAN GIRL	2	SCREAM	4
LOOKIN' THROUGH THE WINDOWS	0	SHAKE YOUR BODY (DOWN TO THE GROUND)	0
LOVELY ONE	0	SHE'S OUT OF MY LIFE	1
MAMA'S PEARL	0	SHOW YOU THE WAY TO GO	0
MAN IN THE MIRROR	22	SKYWRITER	0
NEVER CAN SAY GOODBYE	1	SMOOTH CRIMINAL	12
NOTHIN' (THAT COMPARES 2 U)	0	STATE OF SHOCK	0
OFF THE WALL	4	STRANGER IN MOSCOW	0
		THE GIRL IS MINE	1

THE LOVE YOU SAVE	0	WANNA BE STARTIN' SOMETHIN'	0
THE WAY YOU MAKE ME FEEL	3	WHO IS IT	0
THEY DON'T CARE ABOUT US	5	WHO'S LOVIN' YOU	0
		WHY	0
THRILLER	71	WILL YOU BE THERE	0
TORTURE	0	YOU ARE NOT ALONE	2
WALK RIGHT NOW	0	YOU ROCK MY WORLD	0

FAMOUS JOES

The following twelve clues each describe a
famous person either born or famously known
as Joe or Joseph. Can you name the person
described by each clue?

2009 winner of *The X Factor*

Author of *Catch-22*

Author of *Heart of Darkness* (1902)

Barack Obama's Vice President

Boxing's Italian Dragon

British dramatist, wrote *What the Butler Saw*

JOE McELDERRY	18
JOSEPH HELLER	17
JOSEPH CONRAD	13
JOE BIDEN	13
JOE CALZAGHE	7
JOE ORTON	1

...Continued

FAMOUS JOES

EastEnders Mickey Miller

Frontman of 'The Clash'

Given name of Pope Benedict XVI

Had a 1968 number 1 with 'With a Little Help from My Friends'

The Soviet Union's 'Man of Steel'

US Senator at the centre of 1950s Communist 'witch-hunts'

JEWELLERY

We are going to show you five anagrams of different types of jewellery. Can you untangle them and tell us the most obscure?

ADMIRING NOD

ANGRIER

GEL BAN

KNEECAP CALLER

USED SNOT

DIAMOND RING	13
EARRING	35
BANGLE	89
PEARL NECKLACE	6
NOSE STUD	3

MOONS OF JUPITER

According to NASA's official website, there are fifty natural satellites (or 'moons') orbiting Jupiter that have been discovered and named as of the start of May 2012. We want you to name the most obscure.

ADRASTEA	3	EUKELADE	0
AITNE	0	EUPORIE	0
AMALTHEA	3	EUROPA	16
ANANKE	0	EURYDOME	0
AOEDE	0	GANYMEDE	17
ARCHE	0	HARPALYKE	0
AUTONOE	0	HEGEMONE	0
CALIRRHOE	0	HELIKE	1
CALLISTO	9	HERMIPPE	0
CARME	0	HERSE	0
CARPO	3	HIMALIA	2
CHALDENE	0	IO	19
CYLLENE	0	IOCASTE	1
ELARA	2	ISONOE	0
ERINOME	0	KALE	0
EUANTHE	0	KALLICHORE	0

KALYKE	0	PASITHEE	0
KORE	0	PRAXIDIKE	0
LEDA	4	SINOPE	0
LYSITHEA	1	SPONDE	0
MEGACLITE	0	TAYGETE	0
METIS	3	THEBE	3
MNEME	0	THELXINOE	0
ORTHOSIE	0	THEMISTO	2
PASIPHAE	0	THYONE	0

Knobbly-kneed Kevin Krantz kicks a kettle over a kennel
while koala Keith kisses his knitted Keira Knightley.

Katie Price – The most infamous jackpot category of all. It was an option on the final board over twenty times and was never chosen. Weird. It has since been retired and can now be found in a glass display cabinet in the National Media Museum.

Kazakhstan – The most famous of the 'stan' countries, and the one that people have the least trouble pronouncing, mainly because Borat was from there. Here are some facts about it. Kazakhstan is the largest land-locked country in the world, but one of the most sparsely populated. It has the world's oldest cosmodrome, should you want to launch a rocket, and its national drink is fermented mare's milk, should you want to keep getting up to go to the loo all night.

Key Cards – Every day Xander and I are given key cards to our dressing rooms, and every day we lose them and find ourselves stranded outside our rooms until we are rescued by a long-suffering runner. I predict that I have lost well over 100 key cards over the years. If, in future episodes of *Pointless*, you see they've forced me to wear my key card on a string around my neck, you'll know why.

Knobstick – Probably the best word I've ever had to say on *Pointless*. It was in the round 'Words Beginning and Ending in K'. It means, of course, a cane with a rounded knob on the end, or a person refusing to join a strike. It's really good fun to say. Try it at Christmas dinner; I promise you your mum won't mind.

Kurdistan – Yes, it's a place, yes it sounds like Kyrgystan (see **Kyrgystan**) and a bit like Kazakhstan (see **Kazakhstan**) but I'm afraid it's not a sovereign state that is a member of the UN in its own right (see **Sovereign State That Is A Member Of The UN In Its Own Right**). That means it is an incorrect answer (see **Incorrect Answers**). Did I mention that I often lose my key cards (see **Key Cards**)?

Kyrgyzstan – A real country of 6 million inhabitants, with expertise in both metallurgy and sugar beet cultivation. Kyrgyzstan is particularly notable for being ten letters long but having just one vowel. It has a vowel percentage of 11.1 per cent, the lowest of any country in the world. In 2009 the UN tried to pass a resolution to send spare vowels to Kyrgyzstan, but it was vetoed by Indonesia, Haiti and Palau. Can you name the country with the highest vowel percentage? With 66.6 per cent vowels, it is, of course, Guinea, just beating Saudi Arabia on 63.6 per cent.

Kyzhygstan – This is exactly the sort of thing people say when they can't pronounce Kyrgyzstan (see **Kyrgyzstan**) but already know deep down that Kurdistan (see **Kurdistan**) isn't a country. They just mumble something that starts with 'K' and ends with 'stan' and hope for the best. It doesn't wash with us.

KEIRA KNIGHTLEY FILMS

Any feature film made for general cinema release, for which Keira Knightley received an acting credit, prior to May 2011. No short films, TV films, documentaries or anything where she has played herself. Voice performances, however, do count.

KNIGHTS IN FILMS

We are going to show you fourteen films and their year of release. Each film features a male star who has been knighted. Can you tell us who they are?

ALIEN (1979)

ARTHUR (1981)

BRIDGE ON THE RIVER KWAI (1957)

DEATH IN VENICE (1971)

DEATH ON THE NILE (1978)

DEMOLITION MAN (1993)

LIVE AND LET DIE (1973)

KNIGHTS IN FILMS

MARATHON MAN (1976)

MY FAIR LADY (1964)

THE GREAT DICTATOR (1940)

THE ROCK (1996)

THE SILENCE OF THE LAMBS (1991)

THE WICKER MAN (1973)

WOMEN IN LOVE (1969)

PRESIDENT KENNEDY

Here are some questions about the 35th President of the United States. We want you to tell us the answers.

City where he died

His political party

Middle name

US state of birth

Wife's first name

WORDS BEGINNING AND ENDING IN 'K'

Any word in the *Oxford English Dictionary* that both begins and ends in the letter 'K'.

Hyphenated words and proper nouns, such as names of people or places, will not be accepted.

KAAK	0	KETJAK	0
KADILIK	0	KETTLEDOCK	0
KAIMA'KAMLIK	0	KHATAK	0
KAKKERLAK	0	KIACK	0
KALMUCK	0	KIBBUTZNIK	0
KAMIK	0	KICK	40
KAPOK	3	KICKBACK	1
KASK	0	KIDDLEYWINK	0
KATHAK	0	KIDDYWINK	0
KAYAK	11	KIDFLICK	0
KEAK	0	KILLBUCK	0
KEBBUCK	0	KILLICK	0
KECK	0	KILOBUCK	0
KEDLOCK	0	KINDLAIK	0
KEEK	1	KINDSFOLK	0
KELEK	0	KINGRICK	0
KELK	0	KINK	13
KENSPECK	0	KINNIKINNIK	0
KERCHUNK	0	KINRICK	0

KIOSK	5	KNUCK	0
KIRK	2	KOLKHOZNIK	0
KITTOCK	0	KOMATIK	0
KLEENEBOK	0	KONAK	0
KLICK	0	KONIAK	0
KLIPBOK	0	KOOK	12
KLUNK	4	KOPDOEK	0
KNACK	12	KOPECK	0
KNAPSACK	1	KORINGKRIEK	0
KNARK	0	KRETEK	0
KNICK	6	KUDLIK	0
KNITWORK	0	KULAK	0
KNOBSTICK	0	KUMBUK	0
KNOCK	31	KWEEK	0
KNOCKBACK	0	KYACK	0
KNOTWORK	0		

POINTLESS FACT

In giving some of the pointless answers to this question Richard become probably the first person to say 'knobstick' on BBC teatime television.

Lottie Langford languidly lugs her laughably limp ladder
and leaves it lying lengthways alongside her lookout.

Lettuce, Types Of

The matchless favourite of all *Pointless* categories ever (but a head in front of Rick Astley) this hails from the days when we had boarded rounds in which seven options were put up, at least one of them incorrect and at least one of them Pointless. These rounds, though little gems, were deemed too easy (which is probably true – that's why we liked them), but that was just the tip of the iceberg cos they were also too expensive, and risked over-heating the tower from the number of pointless answers. So to avoid a rocket from our accounts department, or having to sift through the charred remains of the studio, we abandoned the boarded round. What a crass way of trying to hide lettuce clues in my writing. (Can you spot all the types of lettuce hidden in the paragraph above?

They are Matchless, Butterhead, Round, Little Gem, Iceberg, Cos, Rocket, Chard, Romaine, Watercress – I'm so sorry!)

Lockdown, Monks Of

The ancient Cistercian Priory of Ellestrey once stood on the site of the studio where we record *Pointless*. It was sacked by Henry VIII in 1539 but the ghostly figures of the monks are still said to appear at certain times of the year, most particularly around the Festival of Lockdown, one of the foremost Red Letter Days in the old liturgical calendar. Lockdown fell on the first Sunday after Whitsun (better known to many as Trinity Sunday) and was tradi- tionally the day on which the strict feudal hierarchy of the priory and the village of Ellestrey was relaxed. This custom was to allow even the humblest citizen to approach the abbot to repair any grievance or injustice of the previous year. The monks came to resent this parity with the citizenry, as it was frequently used by the latter as an excuse to demand monks' privileges and access to the monks' cellar and fish larder. To police this, lines of monks with torches would patrol Ellestrey for the dura- tion of Lockdown, chanting and swinging censers. When parity is achieved on *Pointless* (i.e. we have a tie-break) the spectral chant of the monks of Lockdown is said to be audible, although we have never yet seen the monks processing through the studio (I wouldn't rule it out though – see **Fancy Dress**).

LANDLOCKED COUNTRIES OF THE WORLD

We are looking for any country which has no coastline on any sea or ocean. Countries which border only inland seas and lakes will be accepted. By 'country' we mean any sovereign state that is a member of the UN in its own right as of the beginning of May 2011.

We will not accept 'South Sudan' as an answer as it did not become an independent country until July 2011, after we had polled our 100 people.

AFGHANISTAN	6	LUXEMBOURG	29
ANDORRA	11	MACEDONIA	2
ARMENIA	1	MALAWI	4
AUSTRIA	30	MALI	5
AZERBAIJAN	1	MOLDOVA	0
BELARUS	5	MONGOLIA	5
BHUTAN	1	NEPAL	13
BOLIVIA	6	NIGER	4
BOTSWANA	2	PARAGUAY	5
BURKINA FASO	0	RWANDA	3
BURUNDI	1	SAN MARINO	2
CENTRAL AFRICAN		SERBIA	4
REPUBLIC	2	SLOVAKIA	9
CHAD	7	SWAZILAND	1
CZECH REPUBLIC	9	SWITZERLAND	48
ETHIOPIA	0	TAJIKISTAN	2
HUNGARY	14	TURKMENISTAN	1
KAZAKHSTAN	1	UGANDA	3
KYRGYZSTAN	2	UZBEKISTAN	2
LAOS	2	ZAMBIA	6
LESOTHO	2	ZIMBABWE	6
LIECHTENSTEIN	7		

FAMOUS PEOPLE FROM LINCOLNSHIRE

We are going to show you twelve clues to famous people past and present who were born in Lincolnshire.

By 'Lincolnshire' we mean anywhere that is now considered part of the historic County of Lincolnshire.

Actor (b.1949) who played John Bayley in *Iris* (2001)

Comedian (b.1958) who formed popular double act with Dawn French

Comedian who has hosted radio show *Just a Minute* since 1967

Comedy actor who plays Jeremy 'Jez' Usborne in *Peep Show*

First Briton to perform a spacewalk

Football goalkeeper who won 61 caps for England between 1972 and 1983

FAMOUS PEOPLE FROM LINCOLNSHIRE

Lyricist (b.1950) who has collaborated with Elton John since 1967

Motorcyle racer (b.1981) who presented *How Britain Worked* in 2012

Poet who wrote 'The Charge of the Light Brigade' in 1854

Politician who served as Prime Minister from 1979 until 1990

Priest who founded The Samaritans in 1953

Shot-putter who twice won the title of World's Strongest Man

LITERARY TITLES FEATURING WEDDING ANNIVERSARY GIFTS

We are going to show you the author and the usual English title of five literary works, each of which features the name of a traditional UK wedding anniversary gift. However, we have removed the name of the anniversary gift.

We would like you to complete the title that you think the fewest of our 100 could get.

_____ Magnolias by Robert Harling

Cat on a Hot ___ Roof by Tennessee Williams

The _____ in the Smoke by Philip Pullman

The _____ Island by R.M. Ballantyne

The Girl with a _____ Earring by Tracey Chevalier

STEEL	58
TIN	87
RUBY	13
CORAL	6
PEARL	48

LOSING SNOOKER WORLD CHAMPIONSHIP FINALISTS

Quite simply we are looking for any player of the modern era who has lost in the final of the Snooker World Championships.

For the purposes of this question we are treating the start of the 'modern era' of the World Championship as being in 1969 when the championship reverted to being a knock-out tournament. So that's any losing finalist from 1969 up to and including 2011.

ALEX HIGGINS	18	JUDD TRUMP	2
ALI CARTER	0	KEN DOHERTY	0
CLIFF THORBURN	6	MARK SELBY	0
DENNIS TAYLOR	3	MARK WILLIAMS	1
DOUG MOUNTJOY	2	MATTHEW STEVENS	0
EDDIE CHARLTON	0	NIGEL BOND	0
GARY OWEN	0	PERRIE MANS	0
GRAEME DOTT	1	PETER EBDON	4
GRAHAM MILES	0	RAY REARDON	8
JIMMY WHITE	25	SHAUN MURPHY	0
JOE JOHNSON	0	STEPHEN HENDRY	14
JOHN HIGGINS	7	STEVE DAVIS	42
JOHN PARROTT	7	TERRY GRIFFITHS	2
JOHN PULMAN	0	WARREN SIMPSON	0
JOHN SPENCER	0		

Melvin Morse, a melancholy, misguided and mateless
moose, moves and moosehandles his mattress
from under the mistletoe.

Mack, Lee – Surely the unluckiest contestant in *Pointless* history. Lee – one of the loveliest, funniest men you could ever hope to meet – came up to the show with his wife, and with his kids, Arlo and Louie, who are huge fans. It took him three hours to get to the studio thanks to traffic and a blinding rainstorm. We immediately rushed him onto set where he joined his playing partner, his TV dad Bobby Ball. The question 'Words Ending in SON' appeared. Bobby, whose exploits we'll hear even more about later (see **Six Hundred Club**) gave the still-inexplicable answer 'Appleson' and scored 100 points. Everyone else gave perfectly acceptable answers, so by the time the action returned to Lee, he had already lost. He got back in his car with his wife and disappointed children, and drove the three hours home.

Make-up – The make-up room has a number of functions. First, it is the place where my and Xander's ageing faces are given a veneer of respectability (for the many people who ask, my foundation is 'Veneer of Respectability'. Second, it is where you discover every single bit of gossip about the crew. Actually, not every bit; if you want gossip about Debbie, Pauline, Lisa or Nana, who actually work in make-up, then you have to go to Wardrobe (see **Wardrobe**). Third, and most importantly, it's where we are just before recording every day, and it's a room always filled with laughter.

McFly – We love McFly on *Pointless*. They have all been on, though it has to be said, they all failed very badly, except Harry, who seems to be the brains of the outfit. We did let them play a song however, an honour so far also conferred only on Wizzard, Right Said Fred, The Beautiful South and, greatest of all, Nul Points (see **Nul Points**). I know I live near Harry from McFly, first because he gazumped a friend of mine on his house, and second because I often bump into him in Nando's.

Miller, Ben – The former comedy partner of Alexander Armstrong (see **Alexander Armstrong**), Ben has since gone on to much greater things, building an extraordinarily successful and lucrative career on stage and screen. From *Death in Paradise* to *What We Did On Our Holidays* Ben certainly hasn't looked back since splitting with Xander! Most critics agree that this is due to Ben's unique combination of charisma, perfect comic timing and acting brilliance. He is widely acknowledged as the strongest link in the *Armstrong & Miller* show, bringing flashes of genius to the workaday, strongly competent performances of Armstrong. Writer, performer, raconteur and all-round terrific guy, everything Ben touches turns to gold. Although he did get knocked out in the first round of *Pointless*.

Min Je Vic – The Czech Republic version of *Pointless*. Sample questions: 'Czech Football Teams', 'Czech Number One Singles', 'Winners Of I'm A Czech Celebrity, Get Me Out Of Here', 'Winners Of The Great Czech Bake Off', 'Czech Cities Without A "Z" In Their Name' and 'Something Or Other About Ice Hockey'.

Mint Tea – In the short recording breaks between each round on *Pointless* (see **Poop Deck**) Xander and I like nothing more than a refreshing mint tea. Unfortunately, in the very first series I spilt some down my shirt and we are now made to drink out of child-proof Tommee Tippee cups. This is not a joke.

Mitchell & Webb – Of course no discussion of Ben Miller (see **Miller, Ben**) could be complete without discussing David Mitchell and Robert Webb. As we always mention on the show, Mitchell & Webb were so successful and well-loved because they were both brilliantly funny, as opposed to the 50/50 situation with Armstrong & Miller. And as I also often say, this is not me being mean to Xander; it is just very calmly and very politely pointing out his limitations as an actor, writer and comedian. He is a very good singer though.

Monks – (See **Lockdown, Monks Of**)

MADONNA SINGLES WITH THREE-WORD TITLES

We are looking for the name of any UK Top 40 hit single for Madonna that has three words in its title according to the Official Charts Company.

For the purposes of this question we are treating contractions – that is, words with apostrophes such as 'She'll', 'I'm', 'Won't' etc. – as single words. We are not accepting the single 'Living for Love', which came out after this question was put to our 100 people.

FOOTBALL MANAGERS

We are going to show you twelve clues to facts about football managers and coaches. We would like you to tell us their names, please.

Coach of France when they won the FIFA World Cup in 1998

Ex-Newcastle manager, his 1996 on-air rant included the outburst 'I will love it if we beat them. Love it!'

Former England manager, bought a 51 per cent controlling interest in Portsmouth FC for £1 in 1997

Frenchman who took over at Arsenal in 1996

Italian who was appointed England manager in 2007

Managed England to World Cup glory in 1966

...Continued

FOOTBALL MANAGERS

Managed Leeds United for just forty-four days in 1974

Manager of Aston Villa when they won the European Cup in 1982

Sacked as Celtic Head Coach in February 2000 after just eight months in charge

Spaniard appointed Bayern Munich manager in 2013

Took over from Bill Shankly as Liverpool manager

Won a World Cup as a player in 1974 and as a coach for West Germany in 1990

BRIAN CLOUGH	18
TONY BARTON	0
JOHN BARNES	5
PEP GUARDIOLA	10
BOB PAISLEY	6
FRANZ BECKENBAUER	13

MARILYN MONROE

Here is a list of clues to facts about people and things connected with Marilyn Monroe. We'd like you to give us the most obscure answer that you know.

Actress who played her in *My Week with Marilyn*

First covergirl on this magazine, first published in 1953

Last completed film

President to whom she famously sang 'Happy Birthday'

Song written in her honour by Elton John

MINISTERS OF STATE

We are looking for any politician who has held at least one of the big four Great Offices of State, since the first cabinet formed after the 1979 general election, until the cabinet formed after the election in 2010.

The positions are: Prime Minister, Chancellor of the Exchequer, Home Secretary and Foreign Secretary.

ALAN JOHNSON	0
ALISTAIR DARLING	10
CHARLES CLARKE	0
DAVID BLUNKETT	4
DAVID CAMERON	40
DAVID MILIBAND	1
DAVID WADDINGTON	0
DOUGLAS HURD	3
FRANCIS PYM	0
GEOFFREY HOWE	6
GEORGE OSBORNE	21
GORDON BROWN	41
JACK STRAW	12
JACQUI SMITH	1
JOHN MAJOR	33
JOHN REID	2

KENNETH BAKER	0
KENNETH CLARKE	5
LEON BRITTAN	1
LORD (PETER) CARRINGTON	1
MALCOLM RIFKIND	0
MARGARET BECKETT	0
MARGARET THATCHER	38
MICHAEL HOWARD	1
NIGEL LAWSON	11
NORMAN LAMONT	2
ROBIN COOK	3
THERESA MAY	14
TONY BLAIR	49
WILLIAM HAGUE	7
WILLIAM WHITELAW	1

A nostalgic Noah nibbles nachos on a narrowboat while neglecting the nuances of nautical navigation.

Not Really Knowing What To Say – This is a style of delivery I have taken years to develop, refine and master. I wheel it out at various points during a *Pointless* record (see **Jobs**, **Miller, Ben** and **Mitchell & Webb**), and you can recognise its deployment by the thousand-yard-stare and awkward smile that accompany it.

Nul Points – The Eurovision tribute band that Richard and I thought we might just about get away with at the end of our Eurovision special in 2013. It was a kind of Pet Shop Boys rip-off, with Richard taking the Chris Lowe role and me taking that of Neil Tennant. The verse was a blatant steal from Donna Summer's 'Hot Stuff' with a mid-verse riff that once belonged to Human League; however, it was all crafted around the *Pointless* theme tune (see **Bow-dow-now-now-now**) and so we felt we were on pretty safe ground. There were several requests for us to release the song on iTunes (including from our esteemed broadcaster) but Richard and I felt that when the moment came for that kind of caper, why not get a real shark and see if we could jump over that.

SQUARES ON A MONOPOLY BOARD CONTAINING 'N'

We are looking for the name of any square on the Monopoly board that contains the letter 'N'.

To clarify, we mean the classic board of the version sold in Britain, with London place names on it. We are including all forty squares around the perimeter of the board, as long as it contains the letter 'N'.

BOND STREET	29	MARYLEBONE STATION	18
CHANCE	11	NORTHUMBERLAND AVENUE	5
COMMUNITY CHEST	10	OLD KENT ROAD	33
COVENTRY STREET	9	PARK LANE	34
EUSTON ROAD	6	PENTONVILLE ROAD	11
FENCHURCH STREET STATION	18	REGENT STREET	20
FREE PARKING	5	STRAND	14
INCOME TAX	1	THE ANGEL ISLINGTON	19
KINGS CROSS STATION	19	VINE STREET	15
LIVERPOOL STREET STATION	5	IN JAIL/JUST VISITING	0
		ELECTRIC COMPANY	0

NOVELS WITH A NAME IN THEIR TITLES

We are going to show you the titles under which fourteen well-known novels were published. We have removed a personal first name from each title – please tell us what the first name is.

_____ (AUSTEN)

_____ AND THE CHOCOLATE FACTORY (DAHL)

_____ OF GREEN GABLES (MONTGOMERY)

_____ THE OBSCURE (HARDY)

_____'S CHOICE (STYRON)

_____'S ROOM (WOOLF)

_____'S WEB (WHITE)

EMMA	31
CHARLIE	77
ANNE	66
JUDE	27
SOPHIE	37
JACOB	2
CHARLOTTE	53

NOVELS WITH A NAME IN THEIR TITLES

ALIAS _____ (ATWOOD)

I, _____ (GRAVES)

LORD _____ (CONRAD)

LUCKY _____ (AMIS)

MASTER _____ (BAINBRIDGE)

OSCAR AND _____ (CAREY)

THE _____ PAPERS (AMIS)

GRACE	3
CLAUDIUS	25
JIM	10
JIM	26
GEORGIE	1
LUCINDA	7
RACHEL	3

NEWCASTLE

We are going to show you five clues about the city of Newcastle. We'd like you to tell us the answers.

Annual half-marathon that starts in Newcastle and ends in South Shields

It was home to this 90s BBC police drama starring Jimmy Nail

Name of the largest independent library outside of London

Newcastle United FC's bird-like nickname

Year the Tyne Bridge was officially opened

THE GREAT NORTH RUN	52
SPENDER	11
LIT AND PHIL	0
MAGPIES	59
1928	2

NEIGHBOURS

KYLIE

We're looking for the title of any UK Top 40 single released by Kylie Minogue, up to the start of August 2013, which has four words in its title, according to the Official Charts Company. EPs don't count, double A-sides will be counted as separate answers. Collaborations do count as long as Kylie was a named, featured artist.

We will not count any subtitles or words in brackets in the word tally, and where words are contracted, such as 'I've' or 'You've', these count as one word, not two.

KYLIE

GET OUTTA MY WAY	1
GOT TO BE CERTAIN	2
HAND ON YOUR HEART	2
KEEP ON PUMPIN' IT	0
LOVE AT FIRST SIGHT	1
SOME KIND OF BLISS	0
TEARS ON MY PILLOW	1
WHAT KIND OF FOOL	0
WHERE IS THE FEELING?	0
WOULDN'T CHANGE A THING	0
STEP BACK IN TIME	0
I BELIEVE IN YOU	0
COME INTO MY WORLD	0

NEIGHBOURS

GUY PEARCE

We are looking for any feature film given a cinema release, for which the former 'Neighbours' actor Guy Pearce is given an acting credit according to IMDb, up to the beginning of August 2013.

No short films, TV films, documentaries, archive film or uncredited appearances, or films where he played himself. Voice performances do count.

500 EPISODES

We are looking for the name of any character who has appeared in more than 500 episodes of 'Neighbours' up to the beginning of August 2013, according to IMDb.

GUY PEARCE

33 POSTCARDS	0	RAVENOUS	0
A SLIPPING-DOWN LIFE	0	RULES OF ENGAGEMENT	0
ANIMAL KINGDOM	0	SEEKING JUSTICE	0
BEDTIME STORIES	0	THE ADVENTURES OF PRISCILLA, QUEEN OF THE DESERT	16
BREATHE IN	0		
DATING THE ENEMY	0		
DEATH DEFYING ACTS	0	THE COUNT OF MONTE CRISTO	0
DON'T BE AFRAID OF THE DARK	0	THE HARD WORD	0
FACTORY GIRL	0	THE HURT LOCKER	0
FIRST SNOW	0	THE KING'S SPEECH	0
FLYNN	0	THE PROPOSITION	0
HEAVEN TONIGHT	0	THE ROAD	0
HUNTING	0	THE TIME MACHINE	0
I AM YOU	0	TILL HUMAN VOICES WAKE US	0
IRON MAN 3	2	TRAITOR	0
L.A. CONFIDENTIAL	6	TWO BROTHERS	0
LAWLESS	0	WINGED CREATURES	0
LOCKOUT	0	WOUNDINGS	0
MEMENTO	11		
PROMETHEUS	3		

500 EPISODES

ANDREW ROBINSON	0	LIBBY KENNEDY	1
BEN KIRK	0	LOU CARPENTER	4
CALLUM JONES	0	LUCAS FITZGERALD	1
CHARLIE HOYLAND	0	LYN SCULLY	0
CHRIS PAPPAS	0	MADGE BISHOP	24
DANIEL FITZGERALD	0	MICHAEL WILLIAMS	0
DECLAN NAPIER	0	PAUL ROBINSON	20
DES CLARKE	0	PHILIP MARTIN	0
HAROLD BISHOP	25	RINGO BROWN	0
HELEN DANIELS	0	STEPHANIE SCULLY	1
JIM ROBINSON	4	SUSAN KENNEDY	10
KARL KENNEDY	13	TOADFISH REBECCHI	7
KYLE CANNING	0	ZEKE KINSKI	0

Orla Olsen offends an outraged owl while oblivious, an obliging octopus oils the owl's ornate orrery.

Oak Leaf Wine – A contestant once proudly boasted about making his own oak leaf wine. Why? I've no idea. During the first round I rashly predicted that at least one of our players would score 100. I assume it was a round on poetry or something. So confident was I that I vowed to drink oak leaf wine if I was proved wrong. Of course everyone then proceeded to answer perfectly and on the next show I was forced to drink it. And what did it taste like? Well, it tasted like someone had, for no reason whatsoever, decided to make some wine out of oak leaves, even though we already know how to make wine really, really well with grapes. I have not tried it since, and I am now much more circumspect about my predictions.

Obviously – 'Obviously' was the original name for *Pointless* during its early stages of development. It's actually not a bad name for a show so I'm fairly sure we'll recycle it at some point. For the brief time that the show was called *Obviously*, an answer which scored zero points was called a 'Plegazoid'. I think my life would be very different if, every time I walked down the street, people wound down their windows to shout 'Plegazoid!' at me.

Ombudsman – Another of my favourite *Pointless* facts is that there are only two words of Swedish origin in the English language. One is 'Ombudsman'. Can you guess the other?

One Hundred – We are often asked who the famous '100 people' are, and whether it's the kind of group you can apply to be in. The 100 are a cross-section of the British population who are contacted by an online polling company. Some of them, I'm sure, know that they're answering questions for *Pointless*, but others will have no idea (particularly the eleven who didn't recognise Earth). You can't volunteer to be in the 100, because if it was full of clever *Pointless* fans then it would no longer be representative, and there would never be any more pointless answers.

Orville – Our favourite, and certainly best-behaved, celebrity guest is Orville. He's been on twice, both times with Keith Harris for some reason.

Osman, Richard – Me. I'm very much the Orville to Alexander Armstrong's Keith Harris (no, not in that way). It is widely believed that I am very tall, but I'm actually just standing very close to you.

Owls – If you look carefully, the head-to head podiums look like owls. Enormous yellow and blue owls sure, but owls nonetheless.

Oxhapetil – Oxhapetil is my Native Aztec spirit guide. He is invisible to everyone except true believers. He is a source of comfort and solace to me, but is also on hand with interesting facts from time to time. For example, he knows that the other Swedish word in the English language is 'Smorgasbord'. Oxhapetil was an Aztec warrior from the time of the Spanish Conquistadors, and, having been separated from his unit and slain upon the sacred hill of Xucattip, now walks alone in the Eternity of Dreams waiting for salvation. Though when we are not filming, he lives in a very nice bungalow in Hemel Hempstead with his wife Jean.

OLYMPICS MULTI-EVENT DISCIPLINES

We are going to show you a list of four different multi-event sports as featured at the Summer Olympic Games. We'd like you to name any individual event (or discipline) which forms part of at least one of these Olympic sports. We will accept distances alone for running events; however, we will require the name of the discipline (and wherever necessary a distance) for anything else.

Any discipline which features in more than one of these sports, we will only accept as an answer once.

DECATHLON – 10 DISCIPLINES

HEPTATHLON – 7 DISCIPLINES

MODERN PENTATHLON – 5 DISCIPLINES

TRIATHLON – 3 DISCIPLINES

DECATHLON

100M	44
110M HURDLES	15
1500M	18
400M	32
DISCUS THROW	35
POLE VAULT	29

DECATHLON & HEPTATHLON

HIGH JUMP	55
JAVELIN THROW	58
LONG JUMP	61
SHOT PUT	34

HEPTATHLON

100M HURDLES	6
200M	9
800M	24

MODERN PENTATHLON

200M SWIM	1
3KM RUN	0
FENCING	11
RIDING	9
SHOOTING	26

TRIATHLON

10KM RUN	1
1500M SWIM	1
40KM CYCLE	0

OPERAS

We are going to show you the usual English titles of fourteen well-known operas or operettas with one word missing. Please tell us the missing word. The surname of the composer appears in brackets.

_____ GRIMES (BRITTEN)

_____ ON THE BEACH (GLASS)

_____ TELL (ROSSINI)

DIDO AND _____ (PURCELL)

DUKE BLUEBEARD'S _____ (BARTÓK)

HANSEL AND _____ (HUMPERDINCK)

LADY _____ OF THE MTSENSK DISTRICT (SHOSTAKOVICH)

PETER	28
EINSTEIN	6
WILLIAM	70
AENEAS	17
CASTLE	7
GRETEL	90
MACBETH	5

OPERAS

MADAME _____ (PUCCINI)

PORGY AND _____ (GERSHWIN)

RISE AND FALL OF THE CITY OF _____ (WEILL)

THE _____ OF FIGARO (MOZART)

THE _____ OF PENZANCE (GILBERT AND SULLIVAN)

THE CUNNING LITTLE _____ (JANÁČEK)

TRISTAN AND _____ (WAGNER)

OLIVER TWIST

Here are five clues which lead to answers about the novel *Oliver Twist*. Do you know the answers?

Book published in which century

Name of Bill Sikes' dog

Name of the parish beadle

Real name of the Artful Dodger

Written by

007 FILMS

M OR Q

We are looking for the name of anyone who has played either 'M' or 'Q' in any of the twenty-three official James Bond feature films produced by EON.

To be clear, they have to have been referred to as either 'M' or 'Q' in the film and/or in the credits.

DIRECTOR

We are looking for the name of anyone who has directed one or more official James Bond film as of the start of 2013.

SINGER OR GROUP

We are looking for the name of any singer or group who performed the official opening title song of an official Bond film starring Roger Moore.

M OR Q

BEN WHISHAW	1
BERNARD LEE	3
DESMOND LLEWELYN	10
JOHN CLEESE	14
JUDI DENCH	66
RALPH FIENNES	4
ROBERT BROWN	0

DIRECTOR

GUY HAMILTON	0
JOHN GLEN	1
LEE TAMAHORI	0
LEWIS GILBERT	1
MARC FORSTER	0

MARTIN CAMPBELL	0
MICHAEL APTED	0
PETER HUNT	0
ROGER SPOTTISWOODE	0
SAM MENDES	9
TERENCE YOUNG	1

SINGER OR GROUP

CARLY SIMON	4
DURAN DURAN	13
LULU	2
PAUL McCARTNEY AND WINGS	10
RITA COOLIDGE	0
SHEENA EASTON	9
SHIRLEY BASSEY	52

Polar bear Petra pauses while pursuing Paul the panda
and ponders the pretty patterns on the pads of her paws.

Poop Deck – This is the name Richard and I have given to the upper level of the *Pointless* set where Podiums 2 and 4 stand. This name derives from the jaunty railing that swoops up behind it, at once (a) providing a barrier to stop Christopher Biggins from taking a misjudged backwards step and becoming involved with the complex electrics that coil thereabouts, and (b) lending a nautical air to the whole proceedings. In the gap between the second round and the head-to-head in each show, Richard and I like to sit on the two steps leading up to the Poop Deck and drink peppermint tea. There has been talk of us acquiring a couple of captain's hats of the kind seen on barge holidays to complete the atmosphere of maritime ease, but so far we haven't quite got around to it.

Punt – In the grammar of *Pointless* game-play there are essentially two kinds of answer: the Safe Answer and the Punt. The so-called Safe Answer, which can occasionally be very dangerous (see **Befriend**), is generally speaking any answer that you have complete confidence in but that you think will still score low enough to get you through. A Safe Answer will never set the *Pointless* confetti cannon off (this, as far as I'm aware, is a piece of pyrotechnics we do not own) but it might keep you in the game, whereas a Punt can all too often result in an early bath (this is, I fear, another piece of technology we do not own). The Punt, however, is where all of *Pointless*'s fun and piquancy comes from; those moments of blind panic when a contestant knows he or she can't go for the easy, Manchester United, kind of answer, but must stray into the more murky, Blackburn Olympic, territory of specialist (often only half-remembered) knowledge. If a Punt pays off then it's a small triumph for us as a species; we can marvel at the fantastical capabilities of the cerebellum we all carry around within us. If a Punt fails then it will most often lead either to hilarity or to a splendid warm feeling of *schadenfreude*, or both.

One thing is for sure though: in the same way that Thurrock (we are informed) 'Welcomes careful drivers', *Pointless* – if we ever put up signage around its perimeter

– 'Welcomes risk takers'. One of the cardinal sins of *Pointless* (see **Red Card Offences**) is to squander the chance of a safe Punt. When I tell a contestant that they are safely through to the next round no matter what they score and they say, 'I'll play it safe, Alexander, I'm going for Manchester United', the keen of eye will notice a dark look dance across my face for the split-second it takes for me to regain control of my faculties.

PRIME MINISTERS WHO SERVED DURING A QUEEN'S REIGN

We are looking for the name of anyone who has served as UK Prime Minister at any time during the reigns of either Queen Victoria or Queen Elizabeth II up to the start of 2015.

ALEC DOUGLAS-HOME	10	HENRY JOHN TEMPLE, 3RD VISCOUNT PALMERSTON	5
ANTHONY EDEN	13	JAMES CALLAGHAN	34
ARCHIBALD PRIMROSE, 5TH EARL OF ROSEBERY	0	JOHN MAJOR	73
BENJAMIN DISRAELI, THE EARL OF BEACONSFIELD	26	LORD JOHN RUSSELL	0
DAVID CAMERON	80	MARGARET THATCHER	82
EDWARD HEATH	42	ROBERT GASCOYNE-CECIL, 3RD MARQUESS OF SALISBURY	1
EDWARD SMITH-STANLEY, 14TH EARL OF DERBY	0	SIR ROBERT PEEL	4
GEORGE HAMILTON-GORDON, 4TH EARL OF ABERDEEN	1	TONY BLAIR	86
GORDON BROWN	62	WILLIAM GLADSTONE	16
HAROLD MACMILLAN	20	WILLIAM LAMB, 2ND VISCOUNT MELBOURNE	0
HAROLD WILSON	45	SIR WINSTON CHURCHILL	46

PLAYS AND THEIR PLAYWRIGHTS

We are going to show you the titles of twelve plays. We want you to tell us who wrote each play.

A MIDSUMMER NIGHT'S DREAM

A STREETCAR NAMED DESIRE

ARCADIA

EDUCATING RITA

JERUSALEM

LOOK BACK IN ANGER

NOISES OFF

PRIVATE LIVES

THE CARETAKER

THE CRUCIBLE

THE IMPORTANCE OF BEING EARNEST

WAITING FOR GODOT

WILLIAM SHAKESPEARE	81
TENNESSEE WILLIAMS	16
TOM STOPPARD	0
WILLY RUSSELL	15
JEZ BUTTERWORTH	0
JOHN OSBORNE	8
MICHAEL FRAYN	5
NOEL COWARD	12
HAROLD PINTER	10
ARTHUR MILLER	21
OSCAR WILDE	32
SAMUEL BECKETT	16

CHEMICAL ELEMENTS BEGINNING WITH 'P'

We are looking for any chemical element whose English name begins with the letter 'P' as verified by the IUPAC, as at the beginning of May 2011.

PALLADIUM	13
PHOSPHORUS	35
PLATINUM	29
PLUTONIUM	39
POLONIUM	9
POTASSIUM	56
PRASEODYMIUM	1
PROMETHIUM	2
PROTACTINIUM	0

PET SHOP BOYS UK TOP 40 SINGLES

We are looking for the title of any single released by the Pet Shop Boys, or which has them as a featured artist, that reached the Top 40 of the UK chart prior to the beginning of April 2011, including collaborations, but excluding remixes.

We will not accept 'Absolutely Fabulous', which was performed by the Pet Shop Boys with Jennifer Saunders and Joanna Lumley, under the name 'Absolutely Fabulous'.

A RED LETTER DAY	0	I GET ALONG	0
ALWAYS ON MY MIND	7	I WOULDN'T NORMALLY DO THIS KIND OF THING	0
BEFORE	0		
BEING BORING	1	I'M WITH STUPID	0
CAN YOU FORGIVE HER	0	IT DOESN'T OFTEN SNOW AT CHRISTMAS	0
DID YOU SEE ME COMING?	0	IT'S A SIN	9
DJ CULTURE	0	IT'S ALRIGHT	2
DOMINO DANCING	3	JEALOUSY	1
FLAMBOYANT	0	LEFT TO MY OWN DEVICES	0
GO WEST	11		
HEART	3	LIBERATION	0
HOME AND DRY	0	LOVE COMES QUICKLY	1
HOW CAN YOU EXPECT TO BE TAKEN SERIOUSLY?	0	LOVE ETC	1
		MINIMAL	0
I DON'T KNOW WHAT YOU WANT BUT I CAN'T GIVE IT ANY MORE	0	MIRACLES	0
		NEW YORK CITY BOY	0

A querulous queen quashes the quibbles of the quaking quizzmasters over the questionable quality of their quips.

Qatar – Often a good answer, though becoming increasingly well known for hosting international sporting events that probably shouldn't be taking place in such a hot place. They have been accused of bribing officials to land the 2022 World Cup. I couldn't possibly comment, but I'm definitely suspicious that they're hosting the 2025 Winter Olympics. If ever I hear the word 'Qatar' I immediately want to do an 'electric Qatar' pun, in the same way that if a contestant ever says 'Djibouti' I know I'm going to say 'shake Djibouti' and if they ever say 'Beryllium' I will say 'That's a beryllium-t answer.' I can't help myself.

Queen Elizabeth II – Recognised by 92 of our 100 respondents, which makes her more famous than the planet Earth, but less famous than Terry Wogan.

Questions – (See **Answers**)

Question Team – The question team are the awesome beating heart of the *Pointless* machine. No matter how many times people insist to me on Twitter that we've got a question wrong, usually including the hashtags #poorresearch or #sacktheresearcher, every single time I look into it, our question team got it right. This is largely because they are awesomely clever, very, very hard-working, and banned from using Wikipedia as a source for verifying questions. They really are the most wonderful bunch.

Queue – If you come to see *Pointless* being recorded live, and you should, then the fun starts in the queue. Due to a combination of people getting there early to nick the best seats, and the lack of any shelter whatsoever, it is a very good place to get a tan, or, in the unlikely event that it should ever rain, a really good place to enjoy rain.

Quizzes – Most books that have an A–Z have a lot of trouble with 'Q', but we're laughing because we're a 'quiz' that has 'questions'. Even 'X' isn't too bad because of Xander. Though I am looking forward to seeing how he deals with 'Z'. What's he got there? Zimbabwe maybe?

Zinedine Zidane? I think he's going to have real trouble. If I'm honest, I'm very impressed that he hasn't yet rung me up in a panic crying, 'Help me! I've got nothing for Z!' If he does ring I'll remind him we once had 'Zammo' from Grange Hill on *Pointless Celebrities*, but I think that's all I've got. All in all I'm happy I got 'Q' instead.

Quizzlesticks – Complicated quizzes are often compared to the wonderful Mitchell & Webb (see **Mitchell & Webb**) sketch 'Numberwang'. It's a funny sketch, mainly because Mitchell and Webb are such talented writers and performers, a rare combination in a British double act (see **Miller, Ben**). But before 'Numberwang' there was the equally brilliant 'Quizzlesticks' from the wonderful *Adam & Joe Show*. Do seek it out on YouTube. Incidentally, Adam and Joe were another example of a double act with two equally brilliant performers (see **Miller, Ben** again).

MEMBERS OF FAMOUS QUARTETS

Here are the names of six bands that are made up of four members.

We would like you to name any band member from any of the bands. We are looking for the band members with which the band had the majority of hits. We will accept their stage names.

The bands are:

TALKING HEADS

QUEEN

LED ZEPPELIN

COLDPLAY

THE BEATLES

McFLY

COLDPLAY

CHRIS MARTIN	29
GUY BERRYMAN	1
JONNY BUCKLAND	1
WILL CHAMPION	1

QUEEN

BRIAN MAY	43
FREDDIE MERCURY	64
JOHN DEACON	9
ROGER TAYLOR	13

LED ZEPPELIN

JIMMY PAGE	12
JOHN BONHAM	9
JOHN PAUL JONES	6
ROBERT PLANT	17

TALKING HEADS

CHRIS FRANTZ	2
DAVID BYRNE	10
JERRY HARRISON	2
TINA WEYMOUTH	2

McFLY

DANNY JONES	3
DOUGIE POYNTER	7
HARRY JUDD	4
TOM FLETCHER	1

THE BEATLES

GEORGE HARRISON	56
JOHN LENNON	83
PAUL McCARTNEY	80
RINGO STARR	71

'Q' FOODS

We are going to show you a list of clues to types of food and drink whose names either begin with, or contain, the letter 'Q'. We would like you to say what food or drink each clue describes.

Blue cheese made from sheep's milk and aged in limestone caverns

Bunch of mixed herbs added to soups or stews

Classic French dish of chicken braised in red wine

Cocktail of rum, lime juice and sugar

Fruit cordial, dilute to taste

Grain-like seed, staple food in the Andes

ROQUEFORT	9
BOUQUET GARNI	26
COQ AU VIN	38
DAIQUIRI	8
SQUASH	46
QUINOA	16

'Q' FOODS

Mexican spirit, often served with salt and lemon

Savoury egg custard baked in pastry, a speciality of Alsace-Lorraine in France

Seafood, sometimes known as 'calamari'

Small Asian citrus fruit

Thick soup, often made with lobster

Yellow, pear-shaped fruit, mentioned in the poem, 'The Owl and the Pussycat'

QUENTIN TARANTINO

We are going to show you five clues to facts about the film director Quentin Tarantino; we would like you to give us the answer to the most obscure.

Character he played in *Reservoir Dogs*

Decade he was born

He was a special guest director on this 2005 Robert Rodriguez/Frank Miller film

Known as his muse, this actress played The Bride in *Kill Bill: Vol. 1*

Received an Oscar at the 1995 Academy Awards Ceremony for writing this film

QI PANELLISTS

We are looking for the name of anyone who has appeared as a panellist on the TV show *QI*, since it began in 2003 up to the end of Series J in 2013. We will accept panellists who appeared on the Comic Relief and Sports Relief Specials.

For obvious reasons, we will not allow Alexander Armstrong as an answer, nor the show's host, Stephen Fry.

AL MURRAY	3	DR BEN GOLDACRE	0
ALAN DAVIES	27	EDDIE IZZARD	2
ANDY HAMILTON	2	EMMA THOMPSON	1
ANDY PARSONS	1	FRANK SKINNER	1
ANNEKA RICE	0	FRED MACAULAY	0
ARTHUR SMITH	1	GRAEME GARDEN	0
BARRY CRYER	1	GRAHAM NORTON	1
BARRY HUMPHRIES	0	GREG PROOPS	1
BEN MILLER	0	GYLES BRANDRETH	0
BILL BAILEY	12	HELEN	
BRIAN BLESSED	1	ATKINSON-WOOD	0
CAL WILSON	0	HENNING WEHN	0
CHARLIE HIGSON	0	HOWARD GOODALL	1
CHRIS ADDISON	0	HUGH DENNIS	1
CLARE BALDING	1	HUGH LAURIE	1
CLIVE ANDERSON	5	JACK DEE	3
DANIEL RADCLIFFE	4	JACK WHITEHALL	0
DANNY BAKER	1	JACKIE CLUNE	0
DARA Ó BRIAIN	6	JAN RAVENS	0
DAVE GORMAN	1	JASON MANFORD	1
DAVID MITCHELL	11	JEREMY CLARKSON	13
DAVID O'DOHERTY	0	JEREMY HARDY	0
DAVID TENNANT	2	JESSICA STEVENSON	0
DAVID WALLIAMS	0	JIMMY CARR	16
DOM JOLY	0	JO BRAND	23
DOON MACKICHAN	0	JOHN BISHOP	0

JOHN HODGMAN	0	PROF BRIAN COX	1
JOHN LLOYD	0	REGINALD D. HUNTER	3
JOHN SERGEANT	1	RHYS DARBY	0
JOHN SESSIONS	4	RICH HALL	7
JOHNNY VAUGHAN	0	RICHARD COLES	0
JOHNNY VEGAS	6	RICHARD E. GRANT	1
JONATHAN ROSS	0	ROB BRYDON	6
JOSIE LAWRENCE	0	ROBERT WEBB	0
JULIA MORRIS	0	ROGER McGOUGH	0
JULIA ZEMIRO	0	RONNI ANCONA	1
JULIAN CLARY	1	RORY BREMNER	0
KATY BRAND	0	RORY McGRATH	1
LEE MACK	3	ROSS NOBLE	5
LINDA SMITH	1	RUBY WAX	0
LIZA TARBUCK	1	RUSSELL TOVEY	0
MARCUS BRIGSTOCKE	0	SANDI TOKSVIG	10
MARK GATISS	0	SARAH MILLICAN	3
MARK STEEL	0	SEAN LOCK	5
MEERA SYAL	0	SHAPPI KHORSANDI	0
NEIL MULLARKEY	0	SIR TERRY WOGAN	0
NINA CONTI	1	SUE PERKINS	3
PAM AYRES	1	SUSAN CALMAN	0
PETER SERAFINOWICZ	0	TIM VINE	0
PHIL KAY	1	VIC REEVES	1
PHILL JUPITUS	15	VICTORIA COREN	0

Richard rides a rickshaw around the remains of
the ruined Roman ramparts with a rabbit and a rat
in his rucksack.

Radcliffe, Daniel – A virtual love affair has struck up between Mr Radcliffe and *Pointless*. He has made no secret of his feelings for the show, and we in turn like to trumpet abroad how much affection we have for the star of the *Harry Potter* films, *The Woman in Black, Equus, My Boy Jack* and many other triumphant roles on stage and on screens both silver and small. We love Daniel Radcliffe. We don't wish to start rumours but if, at some point in the future, you see Radcliffe walking down a red carpet, possibly at a premiere or some awards show, with *Pointless* on his arm, you are not to be surprised.

Red Card Offences – The idea of a Red Card system on *Pointless* is a relatively new one and certainly was not a move either Richard or I welcomed; however, persistent contravention of basic game-play protocols has meant that tough new measures simply had to be introduced.* At the time of going to press there are only two official Red Card Offences (see **Before My Time** and **Punt**). But other areas we might consider at some point in the future include saying, 'Oh I don't know anything about this subject', and proceeding to get a pointless answer (a move that currently elicits a verbal warning), going for a subject that both can answer when there's a glaringly obvious specialist subject that one contestant could nail (although this 'sending-off offence' becomes self-fulfilling so perhaps needn't be enacted) and claiming 'baking' as a hobby but not bringing in so much as a flapjack for Richard and me.

*Of course, none of this actually means anything – no-one gets sent off on *Pointless* no matter what they've done (see **Jizz**).

Richard – Or Richard Thomas Osman (to give him his full name – see **Osman, Richard**) is the man behind the towering success of *Pointless*; he's why *Pointless* is so much fun to make and therefore he's why it is so much fun to watch. He was also part of the small team of people who came up with idea of *Pointless*. In fact before the first show aired on 24 August 2009 Richard's role in television had been entirely confined to sitting in anonymous poorly-ventilated rooms with writers cooking up ace television formats. And so it would have remained. But from the minute Osman agreed to take the swivel-chair on *Pointless* he has become one of the best-loved figures in broadcasting. He has been recreated in wool, cake mix, acrylic, mixed media, pen and ink, icing sugar, and simple cardboard. He often stands in for Patrick Carney from the Black Keys when he is indisposed (Patrick once stood in for Richard and – but for his strange pronunciation of 'sovereign' – would have been indistinguishable). Richard is 6'7" and supports Fulham Football Club.

WORDS ENDING IN 'RAGE'

We are looking for any word that has its own entry in the *Oxford Dictionary of English* that ends in the letters R-A-G-E. We will not allow hyphenated words, trademarks, abbreviations or proper nouns. We will not accept the word 'rage' itself.

AMPERAGE	1	HARBOURAGE	0
ANCHORAGE	2	LAIRAGE	0
ARBITRAGE	0	LEVERAGE	5
AVERAGE	10	LIGHTERAGE	0
BARRAGE	15	MIRAGE	18
BEVERAGE	6	MURAGE	0
BORAGE	4	OUTRAGE	49
BROKERAGE	1	OVERAGE	1
CELLARAGE	0	PASTURAGE	0
COOPERAGE	0	PEERAGE	3
COURAGE	42	PORTERAGE	0
COVERAGE	4	QUARTERAGE	0
DEMURRAGE	0	SAXIFRAGE	0
DISCOURAGE	6	SEIGNIORAGE	0
DISPARAGE	2	SEWERAGE	5
EFFLEURAGE	0	STEERAGE	0
ENCOURAGE	11	STORAGE	4
ENFLEURAGE	0	SUFFRAGE	3
ENRAGE	29	TEACHERAGE	0
ENTOURAGE	10	UMBRAGE	1
FACTORAGE	0	UNDERAGE	3
FORAGE	14	VICARAGE	2
GARAGE	27		

REAL FILM ROLES

We are going to show you fourteen actors who have played real people in history in films released in the years shown. Please tell us which famous historical person they played.

BEN KINGSLEY (1982)

COLIN FARRELL (2004)

COLIN FIRTH (2010)

DANIEL DAY-LEWIS (2012)

ELIZABETH TAYLOR (1963)

FOREST WHITAKER (2006)

GEORGE C. SCOTT (1970)

REAL FILM ROLES

INGRID BERGMAN (1948)

MERYL STREEP (2011)

NIGEL HAWTHORNE (1994)

PAUL SCOFIELD (1966)

PHILIP SEYMOUR HOFFMAN (2005)

SEAN PENN (2008)

TOM HULCE (1984)

RICHARD III

We are going to show you five clues to facts about the English monarch King Richard III. We'd like you to tell us the answer to the clue you think the fewest of our 100 people knew.

Battle he was defeated at and killed

City where his bones were discovered in 2012

His character says 'Now is the winter of our discontent' in a play written by this playwright

Northamptonshire castle he was born in

Played by this 'Beyond the Fringe' comedian in the first 'Blackadder' series

R.E.M. UK TOP 40 SINGLES

We are looking for the title of any single released by R.E.M., or which has them as a featured artist, which reached the Top 40 of the UK chart.

Singles which reached the Top 40 on more than one occasion will only be accepted once, and where a title was part of a double-A side, we will accept either title as a separate answer. EPs will not be accepted.

ALL THE WAY TO RENO	1
ANIMAL	0
AT MY MOST BEAUTIFUL	1
BAD DAY	3
BANG AND BLAME	1
BITTERSWEET ME	0
CRUSH WITH EYELINER	0
DAYSLEEPER	3
DRIVE	2
E-BOW THE LETTER	1
ELECTROLITE	0
ELECTRON BLUE	0
EVERYBODY HURTS	22
IMITATION OF LIFE	0
IT'S THE END OF THE WORLD AS WE KNOW IT	3
LEAVING NEW YORK	0

A shocked snowman sits and surveys a scandalous scene:
seven shepherds sucking saveloys!

Sequels – The simplest trick in the book when it comes to a *Pointless* film round. Never say *Toy Story* when you could say *Toy Story 2*, and indeed never say *Toy Story 2* when you could say *Toy Story 3*. If you don't know any Will Smith films and someone on another podium has said *Men in Black* then take a punt on *Men in Black 2*. A very good film incidentally. Sometimes it doesn't work. For example, if someone has said *Titanic* for Kate Winslet Films, then *Titanic 2* wouldn't be a great answer. I would also avoid *Schindler's List 2* for Liam Neeson Films. The best name of any film sequel ever is the sequel to the film *Dude, Where's My Car?* Any idea what they called it?

Seriously Dude, Where's My Car? – They called it that.

Sexual Tension – We have discussed the *Brokeback Mountain*-style sexual tension between Xander and myself before. No further comment other than to say how much Xander reminds me of Ross Poldark.

Six Hundred Club – We know all about the Two Hundred Club. We've even had a few members of the Three Hundred Club (200 points, then a further 100 in 'Lockdown' (see **Lockdown, Monks Of**)). But nothing has ever come close to the sheer, monumental disaster that befell one particular episode of *Pointless Celebrities*. On podium 1 we had Cannon & Ball (see both **Appleson** and **Mack, Lee**), and on Podium 2, Bobby Davro and Kenny Lynch. They faced a fairly simple board of pop songs released by acts from outside the UK, with lots of good answers, from Kraftwerk to Shakira. Both teams scored 200 and we went to 'Lockdown', though this was in the days before the monks (see again **Lockdown, Monks of**). They proceeded to give us four more wrong answers each, pushing both of their scores to a Pointless record of 600. Eventually we had to bring in an entirely new question, one about Bruce Forsyth, before the deadlock was finally broken. It was what we always euphemistically call 'a long recording'. Funnily enough, Orville was there that night too, and was very much the voice of sanity.

Sovereign State That Is A Member Of The UN In Its Own Right – The least catchy catchphrase in television. People do tend to be quite shaky on what a country is and what it isn't, and all the following have been given as incorrect answers over the years on *Pointless*: Africa, Cook Islands, Virgin Islands, Christmas Island, Kurdistan (see **Kurdistan**) New Caledonia, Puerto Rico, Siberia, South Pacific and Vatican City (none are countries by our definition). Also incorrect were Zaire (now Democratic Republic of Congo) and Moldavia (now Moldova). Most memorably, from Toyah Willcox, we had Kiev, which was wrong on a huge variety of levels.

Spies – Often people are not allowed to tell us what their specific job is, particularly if they work in the civil service. They give all sorts of excuses for this, but in 100 per cent of cases we know it is because they are a spy. We have had loads of spies on the programme. Not just desk-bound ones, or military intelligence, but real spies who go to casinos and kill evil masterminds in volcanoes. We know that they are spies, because when we ask if they are, they say 'no'. This is absolute basic spy training.

Steve – The most popular name in *Pointless* history, and also the most successful. There have been eleven jackpot winners called Steve. These winners include Steve, Steve, Steve P., Steve, Stephen, Steve and Steve.

Still Excited About 'Z' – Seriously, what is Xander going to do for 'Z'? He can't even do 'Zaire' now. Poor guy. It's just going to be one long essay about zinc or something.

STEVEN SPIELBERG FILMS SINCE 1990

We are looking for any full-length feature film made for cinema release for which Steven Spielberg was credited as 'director', according to IMDb, that had its first release from the beginning of 1990 to the end of 2012.

SPORTING SIBLINGS

We will give you the name of a sports person, along with the sport they play or played. We are looking for the full name of their sibling who also plays or played the same sport professionally.

ANDY MURRAY – TENNIS

BOBBY CHARLTON – FOOTBALL

FRANCESCO MOLINARI – GOLF

GARY NEVILLE – FOOTBALL

JOE DAVIS – SNOOKER

JONNY SEARLE – ROWING

...Continued

SPORTING SIBLINGS

KAREN JOSEPHSON – SYNCHRONISED SWMMING

LEON SPINKS – BOXING

RIO FERDINAND – FOOTBALL

RORY UNDERWOOD – RUGBY UNION

VENUS WILLIAMS – TENNIS

VITALI KLITSCHKO – BOXING

SARAH JOSEPHSON	0
MICHAEL SPINKS	3
ANTON FERDINAND	27
TONY UNDERWOOD	8
SERENA WILLIAMS	73
WLADIMIR KLITSCHKO	14

THE SWINGING SIXTIES

We will show you some questions about the decade of the twentieth century known as 'the swinging sixties'. We want you to tell us the answers.

Act that had the most UK number one singles during this decade

Full name of the model, nicknamed 'The Shrimp'

Name of the Prime Minister for the majority of this decade

Title of the novel that was involved in a high-profile Obscene Publications trial in 1960

US magazine whose cover, on 15 April 1966, proclaimed London – The Swinging City

SHAKESPEARE

TWELFTH NIGHT

We are looking for any of the named characters in *Twelfth Night*. We won't accept characters who are known only by a job title such as 'Page' or 'Servant'.

MUCH ADO ABOUT NOTHING

We are looking for anyone who was credited with an acting role in the 1993 film adaptation of *Much Ado about Nothing*, according to IMDb.

DOUBLE, DOUBLE, TOIL AND TROUBLE

We are looking for the name of any creature that goes into the cauldron as an ingredient during the Witches' 'double, double, toil and trouble' scene in *Macbeth*.

We will only accept the name of the animal as it appears in the text and we will NOT accept any of the human ingredients as an answer, or ingredients from fictional beings.

TWELFTH NIGHT		MUCH ADO ABOUT NOTHING	
ANTONIO	3		
CURIO	0	ALEX LOWE	0
FABIAN	0	ALEX SCOTT	0
FESTE	0	ANDY HOCKLEY	0
MALVOLIO	16	BEN ELTON	0
MARIA	1	BRIAN BLESSED	0
OLIVIA	8	CHRIS BARNES	0
ORSINO	3	CONRAD NELSON	0
SEBASTIAN	2	DENZEL WASHINGTON	1
SIR ANDREW AGUECHEEK	2	EDWARD JEWESBURY	0
		EMMA THOMPSON	19
SIR TOBY BELCH	3	GERARD HORAN	0
VALENTINE	0	IMELDA STAUNTON	0
VIOLA	4	JIMMY YUILL	0

KATE BECKINSALE	1	BAT	21
KEANU REEVES	5	BLIND-WORM	0
KENNETH BRANAGH	20	DOG	12
MICHAEL KEATON	1	FENNY SNAKE	0
PATRICK DOYLE	0	FROG	32
PHYLLIDA LAW	0	GOAT	1
RICHARD BRIERS	4	HOWLET	1
RICHARD CLIFFORD	0	LIZARD	5
ROBERT SEAN LEONARD	0	NEWT	45
		SHARK	0

DOUBLE, DOUBLE, TOIL AND TROUBLE

		TIGER	0
		TOAD	34
ADDER	0	WOLF	1
BABOON	0		

Top trombone tooter Teddy Thomas tackles Tchaikovsky's typically tricky tarantellas on a tiny tinny trumpet.

Thank You Very Much Indeed – The nearest thing I have to a catchphrase. I say it several thousand times a year on the show. Many will find this hard to believe but it wasn't contrived; I simply found myself in a position of being inordinately grateful to various individuals (for answering questions, for turning up to be on our show, for giving pithy explanations about those answers and why they scored the way they did) at several points throughout the show and had no other way of conveying this. And so 'thank you very much indeed' stuck. I don't suppose many would miss it if I suddenly stopped saying it, but I would probably eventually explode from the pressure of bottled-up gratitude and heaven only knows what that would look like.

Tits and Finches – This is the kind of round that makes me glad to be alive. I love tits and finches and have even learnt – courtesy of our bird-table just outside the *Pointless* kitchen – not just how to tell them apart but to identify the different types. There's the goldfinch with its wonderful yellow and black markings and the little twite with its slender brown stripes, the bullfinch with its grey back and the chaffinch with its browner wing. Beautiful though finches are though, I have to confess that at heart I am a tit man.

Tom Thomas, Rev. – One of many stand-out favourites from our contestants over the years, Tom Thomas was a vicar from Manchester who came on with his son. Thomas was tall and academic with a kind, thoughtful face and gentle manner: an archetypal old-school C of E vicar. Thomas Jr struck me as someone who'd had an excellent Second Summer of Love and hadn't really put the ball down since: an archetypal old-skool C of E vicar's son. We even devised a TV detective series based around 'Rev. Tom Thomas' in which he and a chubby nameless sidekick strode around the Peak District looking for clues. Why we thought this likeable cleric should be the subject of a crime-solving drama I now forget. However, that part of the chubby nameless sidekick had my name written all over it (so to speak). I've still got the show outline if any Sunday night drama producers are interested.

Trophy – The *Pointless* trophy has been 'coveted' since the very first read-through of the show. Now this might sound to some like presenters' hyperbole of the kind many shows like to indulge in ('let's see what *fantastic* prizes you could win!'; 'hasn't he been *wonderful* ladies and gentlemen?!') but at no point do we allow ourselves to make claims that we can't substantiate. An early proto-type of the *Pointless* trophy was taken out in a clear glass case with two security guards who weren't allowed to let it out of their sight. We tested its covet-worthiness on one thousand randomly chosen passers-by in Shepherds Bush. The results were astonishing (and an early indicator that we were on to something BIG). Five people out of those polled were 'indifferent' to the trophy, not a single one of them 'disliked' it and the remaining 995 people wished 'strongly' to have it (i.e. 'coveted' it).

This research has been invaluable to me, as it means every time I mention our coveted trophy I can do so with authority as I remember the skirmishes of sheer trophy-lust that broke out whenever we took that small icon out of its special van and pulled off its little blue velvet hood. Contestants are still sometimes surprised to learn that they receive a trophy each when they get through to the final, but such is the level of covetousness that to force two people to share a *Pointless* trophy would be to put all but the strongest friendships under impossible strain.

Twain, Mark – That champagne moment when we have two contestants on the show called Mark (exceedingly rare).

TAKE THAT SINGLES OF THE 90s

We are looking for the title of any Take That single that reached the UK Top 40 singles chart from the beginning of 1990 to the end of 1999.

The single must have been credited to Take That; solo singles released by members of the band will not count here. However, we will accept Take That singles that featured other artists.

TITULAR FEMALE CHARACTERS AND THEIR CREATORS

We're going to show you twelve eponymous female characters from works of fiction. We would like to know the author of the work in which they appear as the title character.

ANNA KARENINA

DAISY MILLER

LITTLE DORRIT

LORNA DOONE

MADAME BOVARY

MAJOR BARBARA

TITULAR FEMALE CHARACTERS AND THEIR CREATORS

MOLL FLANDERS

MRS DALLOWAY

MRS TIGGY-WINKLE

PIPPI LONGSTOCKING

SHIRLEY VALENTINE

TILLY TROTTER

TERRY WOGAN

We are about to show you five clues to facts about the broadcaster Sir Terry Wogan. We would like you to find the answers, and tell us the most obscure, please.

Celebrity game show he hosted, which had a chequebook and pen as a consolation prize

Decade in which he first became host of the Radio Two Breakfast Show

First name of his wife, to whom he often refers as 'The present Mrs Wogan'

His city of birth

Title of the song with which he had a UK Top 40 single in 1978

TV FROM THE USA

SEX AND THE CITY

We would like the name of anyone who has an acting credit for six or more episodes of the television series *Sex and the City*, according to IMDb.

THE SOPRANOS

We would like the name of anyone with an acting credit for thirty-one episodes or more of the television series *The Sopranos*, according to IMDb.

THE WIRE

We would like the name of anyone with an acting credit in thirty-six or more episodes of the television series *The Wire*, according to IMDb.

SEX AND THE CITY

BEN WEBER	0
BRIDGET MOYNAHAN	0
CHRIS NOTH	2
CYNTHIA NIXON	2
DAVID EIGENBERG	1
EVAN HANDLER	0
FRANCES STERNHAGEN	0
JAMES REMAR	0
JASON LEWIS	1
JOHN CORBETT	0
KIM CATTRALL	20
KRISTIN DAVIS	2
KYLE MACLACHLAN	1
LYNN COHEN	0
MARIO CANTONE	0
MIKHAIL BARYSHNIKOV	0
RON LIVINGSTON	0
SARAH JESSICA PARKER	46
SEAN PALMER	0
WILLIE GARSON	0

THE SOPRANOS

AIDA TURTURRO	0
DAN GRIMALDI	0
DOMINIC CHIANESE	0
DREA DE MATTEO	0
EDIE FALCO	2
FEDERICO CASTELLUCCIO	0
FRANK VINCENT	0
JAMES GANDOLFINI	7
JAMIE-LYNN SIGLER	0
JOHN VENTIMIGLIA	0
JOSEPH R. GANNASCOLI	0
LORRAINE BRACCO	2
MICHAEL IMPERIOLI	0
ROBERT ILER	0
SHARON ANGELA	0
STEVE SCHIRRIPA	0
STEVEN VAN ZANDT	0
TONY SIRICO	0
VINCENT CURATOLA	0

THE WIRE

ANDRE ROYO	0
CLARKE PETERS	0
COREY PARKER ROBINSON	0
DEIRDRE LOVEJOY	0
DELANEY WILLIAMS	0
DOMENICK LOMBARDOZZI	0
DOMINIC WEST	4
FRANKIE FAISON	1
IDRIS ELBA	3
J.D. WILLIAMS	0
JIM TRUE-FROST	0
JOHN DOMAN	0
LANCE REDDICK	0
MICHAEL KENNETH WILLIAMS	0
SETH GILLIAM	0
SONJA SOHN	0
WENDELL PIERCE	0
WOOD HARRIS	0

Ursula Underwood unfurls her umbrella and unleashes an ultimatum to uxorious unicyclist Ulrich Unger, unrepentant in his underpants.

U2 – Occasionally we will have a category on *Pointless* which goes very badly. Usually they are about poetry or nineteenth-century literature and we can all just happily shake our heads at the inadequacies of our education system. More spectacular is when we do a pop culture round that collapses utterly. This has memorably happened four times, as 'U2 Top 40 Singles', 'Robert Redford Films', 'Sebastian Faulks Novels' (see **Faulks, Sebastian – The Works Of**) and 'Ralph Fiennes Films' contained an extraordinary nineteen incorrect answers between them. I can only hope that none of them were watching.

United Kingdom – A rarely raised anomaly on *Pointless* is that England, Scotland, Wales and Northern Ireland are not acceptable answers for 'countries' questions, as, by our definition, they all form part of the United Kingdom. If and when Scotland becomes an independent nation then 'Scotland' will be an acceptable answer, while 'England' won't. It will also be confusing for any question like 'UK Cities' and will make the question 'UK Winners of the Wimbledon Men's Singles' much, much harder.

University Students – *Pointless* seems to be very popular among British students, I'm guessing because for them it is essentially breakfast television. We also love having university students on the show, but over the years I have noticed a strange phenomenon. Exactly half the students who appear on the programme are brilliant, and exactly half are terrible. I think this could be a very commercially useful observation and I might start compiling statistics as to which institutions perform best, and then sell the information to UCAS, or to prospective students. I could also be paid hush money by universities whose English students can't name who wrote *The Old Curiosity Shop*. You know who you are.

Upper Warlingham – A recent jackpot round asked for any station on the UK rail network that begins with an 'I' an 'O' or a 'U'. I commented at the time that it's the sort of question that can win you the jackpot on if you live close to a nice, obscure little station. Our plucky contestants missed the jackpot, but emitted a gasp when I went through the pointless answers and mentioned 'Upper Warlingham'. It was their local station, and literally just around the corner from their house. Oops.

Useless High Fives – We see some pretty poor high fives from celebrating *Pointless* contestants, usually due to one member of the pair being over-enthusiastic, or the other member being taken entirely by surprise. If the editors of the show were kind human beings they would edit out these scenes, but, thankfully for all of us, they are not. There is a secret to the perfect high five by the way. You simply have to keep your eye on the other person's elbow. I promise it works; try it.

Uzbekistan – Apart from its rich and varied culture and history, Uzbekistan interests me for two particular reasons. First, it is one of only two doubly landlocked countries in the world (that is, countries which are landlocked by other countries which are also landlocked) and second, it was the birthplace of my favourite named sportsman of all time, Djamolidine Abdoujaparov, the Tour de France sprint cyclist known as the 'Terror of

Tashkent'. Plucky Djamolidine packs an impressive nine syllables and twenty-three letters into his two names, and I admire that enormously. Incidentally, if the 'U' was knocked off the front of 'Uzbekistan' in a high wind, then it would be called 'Zbekistan' and Xander could write about it under 'Z', but, at the time of writing, that hasn't happened. And, by the way, I know only four of you care, but the other doubly landlocked country is Liechtenstein.

US STATE CAPITALS

We are looking for any state capital of any of the fifty states of the USA. Not including Washington DC, which is the national capital, but not a state capital.

ALBANY	5	JEFFERSON CITY	0
ANNAPOLIS	0	JUNEAU	3
ATLANTA	15	LANSING	1
AUGUSTA	5	LINCOLN	0
AUSTIN	10	LITTLE ROCK	4
BATON ROUGE	4	MADISON	1
BISMARCK	1	MONTGOMERY	7
BOISE	3	MONTPELIER	0
BOSTON	20	NASHVILLE	2
CARSON CITY	0	OKLAHOMA CITY	1
CHARLESTON	0	OLYMPIA	0
CHEYENNE	0	PHOENIX	16
COLUMBIA	0	PIERRE	2
COLUMBUS	3	PROVIDENCE	2
CONCORD	0	RALEIGH	0
DENVER	7	RICHMOND	4
DES MOINES	0	SACRAMENTO	16
DOVER	1	SALEM	3
FRANKFORT	0	SALT LAKE CITY	8
HARRISBURG	1	SANTA FE	2
HARTFORD	2	SPRINGFIELD	3
HELENA	1	ST PAUL	0
HONOLULU	2	TALLAHASSEE	7
INDIANAPOLIS	2	TOPEKA	0
JACKSON	5	TRENTON	0

UK NUMBER ONE SINGLES WITH ONE-WORD TITLES

We are going to show you fourteen UK number one singles that have one-word titles. We'd like you to tell us the artists that had the hits in the year shown.

BLOCKBUSTER (1973)

CARS (1979)

FAME (1982)

GOODBYE (1998)

GRENADE (2011)

HEART (1988)

HELLO (1984)

SWEET	25
GARY NUMAN	20
IRENE CARA	13
SPICE GIRLS	4
BRUNO MARS	16
PET SHOP BOYS	0
LIONEL RICHIE	38

UK NUMBER ONE SINGLES WITH ONE-WORD TITLES

HELP! (1965)

LYLA (2005)

MERCY (2008)

STAN (2000)

VINCENT (1972)

VOGUE (1990)

YOUNG (2012)

USAIN BOLT

We are going to show you five clues to facts about Usain Bolt. We would like you to give us the answers.

His meteorological nickname

His training partner who won silver in the 2012 Olympic 100m race

The country in which he was born

The number of Olympic Gold medals he has won, including relays

The record-breaking time included in the title of his autobiography

LIGHTNING BOLT	27
YOHAN BLAKE	5
JAMAICA	56
SIX	10
9.58	2

UNIVERSITY CHALLENGE

THE YOUNG ONES

We are looking for the name of any individual who received an acting credit for the *Young Ones* episode 'Bambi', a parody of *University Challenge*, according to IMDb.

We are not including Motorhead as they are a group rather than an individual.

STARTER FOR TEN

We are looking for the name of any individual who received an acting credit in the 2006 film *Starter for Ten*, according to IMDb.

COLLEGES

We are looking for the specific name of any university or college that has won a standard competitive series of the TV quiz show *University Challenge*, since it began in 1963, up to and including 2013. For cases in which the winner has been a college of a university rather than the university itself, we require both the name of the university and the individual college.

THE YOUNG ONES

ADRIAN EDMONDSON	21	MEL SMITH	0
ALEXEI SAYLE	0	NIGEL PLANER	7
BEN ELTON	1	RIK MAYALL	34
CHRISTOPHER RYAN	1	ROBBIE COLTRANE	0
EMMA THOMPSON	1	STEPHEN FRY	3
GRIFF RHYS JONES	0	TAMSIN HEATLEY	0
HUGH LAURIE	0	TONY ROBINSON	0

STARTER FOR TEN

ALICE EVE	1	JOHN HENSHAW	0
BEN WILLBOND	0	JOSEPH FRIEND	0
BENEDICT CUMBERBATCH	2	KENNETH HADLEY	0
BETHAN BEVAN	0	LINDSAY DUNCAN	0
CATHERINE TATE	0	MARK GATISS	0
CHARLES DANCE	0	NICHOLAS GLEAVES	0
DOMINIC COOPER	0	RAJ GHATAK	0
ELAINE TAN	0	RASMUS HARDIKER	0
GERARD MONACO	0	REBECCA HALL	1
GUY HENRY	0	REUBEN-HENRY BIGGS	0
IAN BONAR	0	ROBERT CAWSEY	0
JAMES CORDEN	0	SIMON WOODS	0
JAMES GADDAS	0	SU ELLIOT	0
JAMES McAVOY	4	SULE RIMI	0
JOE VAN MOYLAND	0	TOM ALLEN	0

COLLEGES

BIRKBECK COLLEGE	0	KEBLE COLLEGE, OXFORD	0
BRADFORD	1	KEELE	0
CHRIST CHURCH, OXFORD	1	LEICESTER	3
CHURCHILL COLLEGE, CAMBRIDGE	0	MAGDALEN COLLEGE, OXFORD	3
CORPUS CHRISTI COLLEGE, OXFORD	0	MERTON COLLEGE, OXFORD	0
DUNDEE	0	NEW COLLEGE, OXFORD	1
DURHAM	8	OPEN UNIVERSITY	1
EMMANUEL COLLEGE, CAMBRIDGE	1	ORIEL COLLEGE, OXFORD	1
FITZWILLIAM COLLEGE, CAMBRIDGE	0	QUEEN'S UNIVERSITY, BELFAST	0
IMPERIAL COLLEGE	2	SIDNEY SUSSEX COLLEGE, CAMBRIDGE	0
JESUS COLLEGE, OXFORD	2		

SOMERVILLE COLLEGE, OXFORD	0		UNIVERSITY COLLEGE, OXFORD	0
ST ANDREWS	3		UNIVERSITY OF MANCHESTER	15
SUSSEX	1		WARWICK	3
TRINITY COLLEGE, CAMBRIDGE	2			

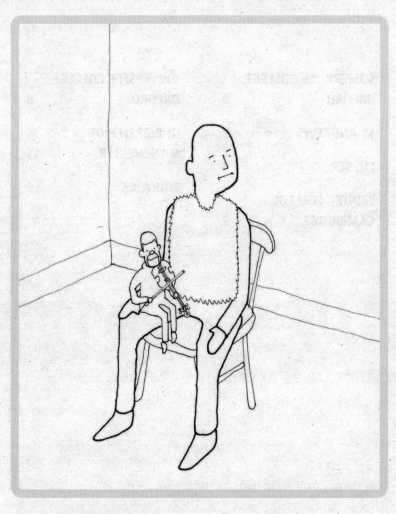

In a vest of vicuña vainglorious ventriloquist Vincent Van Vliet vocalises the vaulting volutes of a virtuoso violinist.

Vanuatu – Along with a handful of others (see **Central African Republic**), Vanuatu rose to early fame as a dead cert pointless answer in any geographical round. That fame then did for its reputation as a guaranteed Get Out Of Jail Card, and saw its score rise up as high as 5. Its popularity was then further enhanced by its inclusion in Richard's and my Eurovision tribute (see **Nul Points**) where its inherent inner rhythm made it perfect as a verbal fill.

Version For Children, Why Don't We Do A – This is a question that is often asked. It would seem to be a brilliant idea: a *Junior Pointless*. It worked perfectly well for Kickstart, after all. But it seems children and young people are currently not allowed to be on game shows – I have absolutely no idea why. When we film *Pointless*, people under eighteen aren't even allowed *into the studio*. This may have more to do with Richard's behind-the-desk-nudity than strict BBC policy but there we are.

Vice – Our interview process and casting sessions for contestants are so thorough that we have to date had no run-ins with anyone's shameful past (touch wood). We have had a 'model' on the show, although – as she pointed out on camera – she'd done 'nothing smutty' (thereby losing me a five-quid bet with Richard). And yes, we did once have Gabriela Irimia on the show and she, as we all know, was once in a very 'unsavoury' double act. With Lembit Öpik.

Victoria Wood – Another person *Pointless* actively adores. It's often asked of Richard and me if we'd ever consider being contestants on the show for charity. Our answer for as long as I can remember has been a firm 'no', until someone put forward the idea of Victoria Wood hosting and Stephen Fry sitting in behind Richard's switched-off laptop. We have now made that the only official condition under which we'd ever step over to the Poop Deck. There is a strong possibility though that we'd be so thoroughly outclassed that we'd never be allowed back.

VOLCANOES AND THEIR COUNTRIES

Here is a list of volcanoes. Can you tell us in which country they are located?

As always, by 'country' we mean a sovereign state that is a member of the UN in its own right.

EYJAFJALLAJÖKULL

COTOPAXI

KRAKATOA

MOUNT MEAGER

MOUNT ARARAT

MOUNT ETNA

ICELAND	27
ECUADOR	0
INDONESIA	12
CANADA	0
TURKEY	5
ITALY	46

VOLCANOES AND THEIR COUNTRIES

MOUNT FUJI

MOUNT RAINIER

MOUNT ST HELENS

POPOCATEPETL

SANTORINI

VESUVIUS

JAPAN	35
USA	5
USA	25
MEXICO	11
GREECE	15
ITALY	40

THINGS IN HISTORY BEGINNING WITH 'V'

We are going to show you twelve clues to historical people and events, all of which start with the letter 'V'. Please give us the answers.

British queen who married Prince Albert in 1840

French Enlightenment writer and philosopher, born François-Marie Arouet in 1694

Name given to 1989 revolution in Czechoslovakia

Name of regime set up in unoccupied France after the French Military collapse in 1940

Palace declared official residence of the court of France by Louis XIV

Roman Emperor, founded Flavian dynasty and began the Colosseum in Rome

THINGS IN HISTORY BEGINNING WITH 'V

Roman poet who wrote the epic poem 'The Aeneid'

Spacecraft launched in 1977 which is the most distant man-made object from the Earth

Surname of Dutch painter of 'Girl with a Pearl Earring'

Surname of Italian composer famous for 'The Four Seasons'

The doge was the highest official of this city state for over a thousand years

This conflict was also known as the Second Indochina War

THE VICTORIAN ERA

We are going to show you five clues to facts about people and culture from the Victorian Era. We would like you to give us the most obscure answer.

BBC series based on works by Elizabeth Gaskell, starring Judi Dench as Matty Jenkyns

Chief engineer of the Great Western Railway

Female cookery writer born in 1836 whose first book sold over 60,000 copies in its first year

First woman awarded the 'Order of Merit'

Name of Sherlock Holmes's landlady

FAMOUS VANS

DICK VAN DYKE

We are looking for the title of any film for which Dick van Dyke has received an acting credit, up to March 2013, according to IMDb. We will not accept short films, documentaries, TV movies or uncredited appearances, but voice performances do count.

DICK VAN DYKE

BYE BYE BIRDIE	0
CHITTY CHITTY BANG BANG	31
COLD TURKEY	0
CURIOUS GEORGE	0
DICK TRACY	0
DIVORCE AMERICAN STYLE	0
FITZWILLY	0
LT. ROBIN CRUSOE, U.S.N.	0
MARY POPPINS	58
NEVER A DULL MOMENT	0
NIGHT AT THE MUSEUM	4
SOME KIND OF A NUT	0
THE ART OF LOVE	0
THE COMIC	0
THE RUNNER STUMBLES	0
TUBBY THE TUBA	0
WHAT A WAY TO GO!	0

FAMOUS VANS

ROBIN VAN PERSIE

We are looking for the name of any club or national team that the footballer Robin van Persie scored a goal against while playing for Arsenal or Holland during the 2011/12 season, which was his last season at Arsenal.

ROBIN VAN PERSIE

AC MILAN	0
ASTON VILLA	5
BLACKBURN ROVERS	0
BOLTON WANDERERS	0
BORUSSIA DORTMUND	0
CHELSEA	20
EVERTON	4
GERMANY	0
LIVERPOOL	15
MANCHESTER UNITED	38
NEWCASTLE UNITED	4
NORTHERN IRELAND	0
NORWICH CITY	1
QUEENS PARK RANGERS	1
SAN MARINO	0
STOKE CITY	2
SUNDERLAND	1
SWANSEA CITY	0
TOTTENHAM HOTSPUR	12
UDINESE	0
WEST BROMWICH ALBION	2
WIGAN ATHLETIC	1
WOLVERHAMPTON WANDERERS	0

FAMOUS VANS

VAN MORRISON

We are looking for the title of any single by Van Morrison that has reached the Top 75 in the UK chart, up to the end of April 2013, according to the Official Charts Company. We will accept both solo singles and collaborations where Van Morrison was a named artist.

We won't accept 'Brown Eyed Girl', since it only entered the charts as a re-release after our 100 people had been asked.

VAN MORRISON

BACK ON TOP	0
BRIGHT SIDE OF THE ROAD	0
DAYS LIKE THIS	0
GLORIA	4
HAVE I TOLD YOU LATELY	4
HEY MR DJ	0
NO RELIGION	0
PRECIOUS TIME	0
THE HEALING GAME	0
WHENEVER GOD SHINES HIS LIGHT	0

Wally Wishart, a wandering wizard in a worsted waistcoat and waders, waits by a waterhole while his wand is washed by Warren, a wistful waiter.

Warden Park – My old school. We have now had two pairs of contestants who also went to Warden Park and their results were as follows. Knocked out in round 1, knocked out in round 1, knocked out in round 1, knocked out in round 1. We then had a contestant who was a teaching assistant at Warden Park. His performance? Knocked out in round 1, knocked out in round 1. To make matters worse we had a contestant on from our local rivals, 'Oathall', and they reached the final. I am slightly worried that this might come up at Warden Park's next OFSTED inspection.

Wardrobe – 'Wardrobe' is run by Sharon and she makes sure that we look smart, but also that the contestants look their best too. Contestants all bring five possible outfits.

Some outfits, particularly those with close patterns, can 'strobe' on camera and can't be used, so Sharon and her assistants hold them all up to the cameras during recording breaks and then choose the best. Or in some circumstances they choose the least worst. The big rule is no logos and no branding, but there is no rule against eye-wateringly bright Hawaiian shirts.

Warm-ups – Every audience comes to watch two shows (free tickets from sroaudiences.com), and before the shows and during the short breaks they are entertained by our warm-up artists. I know this sounds like your idea of hell, but anyone who has been to a recording, especially those who come regularly, will tell you we have the funniest, nicest, warmest, warm-up artists in the business. Our three regulars are Mark Olver, Fin Taylor and Andrew Bird and they are all fantastic, though Fin is so young he recently refused to believe that a 'Snickers' was once called a 'Marathon'.

Watkins, Elaine – My attempt to launch a child-friendly puppet during our Kids TV *Pointless Celebrities* special was a red furry monster called Professor Elaine Watkins, Head of the Engineering Faculty at Brunel University. She failed to catch on.

Well Done If You Got That At Home – People get genuinely upset if they've got a great answer, or have gone through a whole board at home, and I don't say 'well done if you got that at home'. Just so long as you know I can't always say it, but I am always thinking it.

What Would You Spend The Money On? – This is one of Xander's. My favourite answers over the years have been 'I'm going to spend the money on a display cabinet for my *Pointless* trophy' and 'I'm going to spend it on a full working model of Dalek'. This was made even better by the look on his girlfriend's face, which perfectly conveyed the emotion 'He really is you know.'

William Tell – Another great moment in *Pointless* history. When Michael was asked, 'Which William was the playwright who wrote Hamlet', he thought for a moment then confidently replied, 'William Tell'. The only good news in this story is that Michael didn't go to Warden Park (see **Warden Park**).

Woody Allen Films – Woody Allen has always cast hugely famous actors in commercially unsuccessful films. This of course creates the perfect storm for pointless answers in film categories. From Leonardo DiCaprio in

Celebrity through Julia Roberts in *Everyone Says I Love You*, Liam Neeson in *Husbands and Wives* and Jodie Foster and Madonna in *Shadows and Fog*. If you are going to revise two things thoroughly before appearing on *Pointless*, I would suggest Grand Slam tennis winners and the casts of Woody Allen films. Don't get them mixed up though.

WORDS ENDING IN 'ROW'

We are looking for any single word with its own entry in the *Oxford Dictionary of English* that ends in the letters R-O-W. As always, no hyphenated words, proper nouns or trademarks, abbreviations or initialisations. Obviously, we will not accept the word 'row' itself.

ARROW	43	MIDDLEBROW	1
BARROW	40	MONOBROW	1
BORROW	35	MORROW	11
BROW	54	NARROW	28
BURROW	21	OUTGROW	2
COCKCROW	2	OVERGROW	1
CROW	56	OVERTHROW	2
DOWNTHROW	0	PROW	21
ESCROW	3	REGROW	2
EYEBROW	9	RESTHARROW	0
FARROW	14	SCARECROW	9
FENCEROW	0	SEROW	1
FROW	3	SORROW	32
FRUITCROW	0	SPARROW	13
FURROW	19	STROW	2
GROW	47	THROW	25
HARROW	30	TOMORROW	32
HEDGEROW	20	TROW	7
HIGHBROW	4	UPTHROW	0
INTERGROW	0	WHEELBARROW	9
LOWBROW	2	WINDROW	1
MARROW	37	YARROW	6

FOOTBALLERS AND THEIR 'WAGS

We are looking for the names of the footballers who married these women in the year stated.

ABIGAIL CLANCY, 2011

ALEX CURRAN, 2007

CARLY ZUCKER, 2009

CLAUDINE PALMER, 2008

COLEEN McLOUGHLIN, 2008

JOY BEVERLEY, 1958

LEANNE WASSELL, 2009

LOUISE NURDING, 1998

SHEREE MURPHY, 2003

SIMONE LAMBE, 2008

TONI POOLE, 2007

VICTORIA ADAMS, 1999

PETER CROUCH	38
STEVEN GERRARD	33
JOE COLE	16
ROBBIE KEANE	3
WAYNE ROONEY	80
BILLY WRIGHT	2
WES BROWN	0
JAMIE REDKNAPP	40
HARRY KEWELL	16
MICHAEL BALLACK	0
JOHN TERRY	8
DAVID BECKHAM	78

WALES

Here are five questions about people, places or things related to Wales. We want you to give us the answers.

CAPITAL CITY

HIGHEST MOUNTAIN

LARGEST NATURAL LAKE

PATRON SAINT

SMALLEST NATIONAL PARK

CARDIFF	91
SNOWDON	48
LAKE BALA	11
ST DAVID	69
PEMBROKESHIRE COAST	3

'DOCTOR WHO'

THE MASTER

We are looking for the name of any actor who is credited on screen as playing The Master in the television series *Doctor Who* – by which we mean either the original series (1963–1989), the 1996 TV film or the revived series 2005 onwards.

We are not counting Michelle Gomez, who played a female incarnation of the Master, called Missy, after this question was put to our 100 people.

COMPANIONS

We are looking for the name of anyone who played or voiced a character during Tom Baker's tenure as Fourth Doctor on the show between 1974 and 1981, who is listed on the 'Companions' page of the BBC's Classic Series website. We are looking for the actors' names, not the characters' names.

THE MASTER

ANTHONY AINLEY	1
DEREK JACOBI	1
ERIC ROBERTS	3
GEOFFREY BEEVERS	0
GORDON TIPPLE	0
JOHN SIMM	15
PETER PRATT	0
ROGER DELGADO	3

COMPANIONS

DAVID BRIERLEY	0
ELISABETH SLADEN	6
IAN MARTER	0
JANET FIELDING	0
JOHN LEESON	0
JOHN LEVENE	0
LALLA WARD	0
LOUISE JAMESON	3
MARY TAMM	2
MATTHEW WATERHOUSE	0
NICHOLAS COURTNEY	1
SARAH SUTTON	0

'DOCTOR WHO'

We are looking for the title of any full-length episode of *Doctor Who* since the series relaunched in 2005 up until Matt Smith's final regular episode in December 2013. We are counting the titles of the feature-length specials, but we are NOT counting mini-episodes, or teaser prequels.

TITLES

Title	
42	1
A CHRISTMAS CAROL	0
A GOOD MAN GOES TO WAR	0
A TOWN CALLED MERCY	0
ALIENS OF LONDON	0
AMY'S CHOICE	0
ARMY OF GHOSTS	1
ASYLUM OF THE DALEKS	0
BAD WOLF	0
BLINK	6
BOOM TOWN	0
CLOSING TIME	0
COLD BLOOD	0
COLD WAR	0
DALEK	0
DALEKS IN MANHATTAN	0
DAY OF THE MOON	0
DINOSAURS ON A SPACESHIP	0
DOOMSDAY	2
EVOLUTION OF THE DALEKS	0
FATHER'S DAY	1
FEAR HER	1
FLESH AND STONE	0
FOREST OF THE DEAD	0
GRIDLOCK	0
HIDE	0
HUMAN NATURE	1
JOURNEY TO THE CENTRE OF THE TARDIS	0
JOURNEY'S END	0
LAST OF THE TIME LORDS	0
LET'S KILL HITLER	0
LOVE & MONSTERS	0
MIDNIGHT	0

The xenial Xander welcomes the exiles from the xanthic xebec into his xyloid xyst.

Xander – Xander is what I have been called all my life apart from between the ages of thirteen and eighteen when everyone at school called me Alex, Fen or Poshboy (yes, even at public school). While I will generally answer to any noise anyone makes if they clearly mean me, Xander was always my name at home and so, to this day, when I hear 'Xander' I am hearing the voice of a friend (or better, a 'friend'). It pleases me beyond words that I get called Xander on *Pointless* and it is another of the many things that make me feel warm and fuzzy on set (see **Jumpers**). You could be forgiven (and in fact you are) if you thought Xander began with a 'Z' but it doesn't. Up there with Xenophobe and Xylocarp, it is a proud example of the 'for X read Z' rule.

XYZ COUNTRIES

We are looking for the name of any country whose common English name includes the letter 'X' and/or 'Y' and/or 'Z'. By 'country' we mean any sovereign state that is a member of the UN in its own right as of the beginning of April 2011.

AZERBAIJAN	1	MYANMAR	0
BELIZE	1	NEW ZEALAND	21
BOSNIA AND HERZEGOVINA	0	NORWAY	8
BRAZIL	17	PARAGUAY	14
CYPRUS	1	SEYCHELLES	0
CZECH REPUBLIC	6	SWAZILAND	3
EGYPT	8	SWITZERLAND	6
GERMANY	19	SYRIA	2
GUYANA	0	TANZANIA	19
HUNGARY	10	THE FORMER YUGOSLAV REPUBLIC OF MACEDONIA	0
ITALY	14	TURKEY	7
KAZAKHSTAN	2	URUGUAY	0
KENYA	4	UZBEKISTAN	5
KYRGYZSTAN	0	VENEZUELA	4
LIBYA	6	YEMEN	27
LUXEMBOURG	9	ZAMBIA	47
MALAYSIA	2	ZIMBABWE	36
MEXICO	13		
MOZAMBIQUE	7		

EXPLORERS AND THEIR FIRST NAMES

We're going to show you fourteen surnames of famous explorers followed by the years they were alive. Please tell us by which first name they are usually known.

AMUNDSEN (1872–1928)

CARTIER (1491–1557)

COLUMBUS (1451–1506)

COOK (1728–1779)

DRAKE (c.1540–1596)

FLINDERS (1774–1814)

HILLARY (1919–2008)

ROALD	19
JACQUES	1
CHRISTOPHER	87
JAMES	40
FRANCIS	72
MATTHEW	6
EDMUND	68

EXPLORERS AND THEIR FIRST NAMES

LIVINGSTONE (1813–1873)

MAGELLAN (c.1480–1521)

POLO (c.1254–1324)

RALEIGH (c.1552–1618)

SHACKLETON (1874–1922)

TASMAN (c.1603–1659)

VESPUCCI (1451–1512)

DAVID	28
FERDINAND	11
MARCO	76
WALTER	93
ERNEST	31
ABEL	7
AMERIGO	12

EXTREME WEATHER

We're going to show you five clues to facts about things connected to weather. We would like you to tell us the answers.

A Pluviometer is used to measure this aspect of the weather

Century of Britain's worst recorded storm, which killed over 8,000 people

Country in which there was a volcanic eruption that closed airspace in 2010

Name of BBC weatherman who famously said there was no hurricane on its way on the eve of the Great Storm of 1987

Name of the 2006 Oscar-winning documentary about climate change

X

To see whether you have been paying attention across the previous twenty-three letters, we are now going to ask a special question unique to this book.

We want you to name any pointless answer in this book that contains the letter 'X' – obviously we haven't put this question to any of our 100 in this form, but every answer has already been pointless when it was an answer of another question – see how many you can remember.

ASTERIX AND THE VIKINGS

HOW OBELIX FELL INTO THE MAGIC POTION (WHEN HE WAS A LITTLE BOY)

ASTERIX THE GLADIATOR

ASTERIX AND THE NORMANS

ASTERIX AND THE LAUREL WREATH

ASTERIX AND THE GREAT CROSSING

ASTERIX AND THE CHIEFTAIN'S SHIELD

ASTERIX AND THE BIG FIGHT

ASTERIX AND THE BANQUET

ASTERIX AND OBELIX'S BIRTHDAY

CROXLEY

NUMBERSIXVALVERDE

OXO

NEUCHATEL XAMAX

ALEX HYDE-WHITE

ALEXEI SAYLE

ISHAQ BUX

PAUL MAXWELL

REX NGUI

PRAXIDIKE

THELXINOE

HOW CAN YOU EXPECT TO BE TAKEN SERIOUSLY?

RUBY WAX

SAXIFRAGE

ALEX LOWE

ALEX SCOTT

ALEXEI SAYLE (FOR THE SECOND TIME IN THIS BOOK!)

CORPUS CHRISTI COLLEGE, OXFORD

KEBLE COLLEGE, OXFORD

MAGDALEN COLLEGE, OXFORD

MERTON COLLEGE, OXFORD

SIDNEY SUSSEX COLLEGE, CAMBRIDGE

SOMERVILLE COLLEGE, OXFORD

UNIVERSITY COLLEGE, OXFORD

THE GOD COMPLEX

THE LAZARUS EXPERIMENT

Yangchen, a yappy Yeti, yomps to Yeovil to yell at a youthful yeoman for yanking a yawning yachtsman's yawl.

Yellow – There is a *Pointless* board game; it is not as good as the book, but nonetheless it exists. It takes the questions and answers from *Pointless*, but it doesn't have my super-useful explanations of what the exact question is, and this is a flaw. For example, 'UK Top 40 Singles with the Word "Yellow" in the Title'. Virtually everyone thinks of 'Yellow' by Coldplay, and then is understandably annoyed that it's not on the card. But that's because, as I would always helpfully explain in the studio, we never accept an answer which has been mentioned in the question. So no 'Yellow' for singles with yellow in the title, no 'Harry Potter' for characters in the Harry Potter films, and no 'Ice' for words ending in 'ICE'.

Yellow – The colour of the podium that the lowest

scorers stand behind in the head-to-head. The one that looks like a yellow owl (see **Owls**) as opposed to a blue owl (see **Owls** unless you just did). We call them the 'Golden Couple' because the 'Yellow Couple' sounds less impressive.

Yellow – The sixth-longest river in the world after the Nile, Amazon, Yangtze, Mississippi/Missouri and Yenisei.

Yenisei – The fifth-longest river in the world, but I bet you hadn't heard of it until just now.

Yesterday – Now, here's another little *Pointless* trade secret, and once you spot it, you'll never miss it again. We are banned from ever saying 'yesterday' on the show. So whenever we refer to the previous show, we always say 'last time'. This is because we're never sure on exactly which day of the week the episode is going to be shown, and your mind would be blown if we were ever to refer to 'yesterday' on a Monday show. This leads neatly to the fact that in the world of *Pointless* the most covered pop song in history is 'Last Time' by The Beatles.

Yuletide Greetings – Well, that's it from me. All that remains is to thank you for reading and to hope you're having a lovely Christmas. Whether you are reading this in the toilet, in the spare room because your mum has given Uncle Keith your room (that's going to need an airing), or simply sitting on the sofa with your family and a glass of wine, desperately trying to avoid the *Downton Abbey* Christmas Special, all that remains is to sit back, relax, and enjoy Xander attempting to write something even vaguely relevant for 'Z'.

UK CITIES WITH A 'Y' IN THEIR NAME

Quite simply we want you to name any of the ten UK cities that have the letter 'Y' in their name. Obviously we are not counting the word 'City' as part of their name.

CANTERBURY	13
COVENTRY	9
DERBY	12
ELY	4
DERRY/LONDONDERRY	5
NEWCASTLE-UPON-TYNE	4
NEWRY	1
PLYMOUTH	11
SALISBURY	12
YORK	54

YEARS IN WHICH THE UK PRIME MINISTER CHANGED

We are going to show you twelve pairs of politicians who have all been UK Prime Minister over the last 100 years. The clues consist of the names of an incoming Prime Minister, and the outgoing PM who was replaced. We would like you to tell us the year those changes happened.

Anthony Eden replaced Winston Churchill

Clement Attlee replaced Winston Churchill

David Cameron replaced Gordon Brown

David Lloyd George replaced Herbert Henry Asquith

Gordon Brown replaced Tony Blair

Harold Macmillan replaced Anthony Eden

1955	7
1945	14
2010	46
1916	4
2007	19
1957	1

YEARS IN WHICH THE UK PRIME MINISTER CHANGED

Harold Wilson replaced Alec Douglas-Home

Harold Wilson replaced Edward Heath

James Callaghan replaced Harold Wilson

Margaret Thatcher replaced James Callaghan

Tony Blair replaced John Major

Winston Churchill replaced Neville Chamberlain

1964	6
1974	8
1976	6
1979	29
1997	33
1940	19

'YELLOW' UK TOP 40 SINGLES

We are looking for the name of any single that charted in the UK Top 40 that contains the word 'yellow' in its title. Titles released as part of a double-A side will be accepted.

This being *Pointless*, we won't accept just 'Yellow' (a Top 40 single by the group Coldplay) as an answer, for obvious reasons.

YOUNG ACHIEVERS

US PRESIDENTS

We are looking for the name of any US president who was under fifty years of age when they were first inaugurated.

TENNIS GRAND SLAM

We are looking for the name of any male or female tennis player who won a Grand Slam singles title in the Open Era before they were twenty years of age. So this is for Grand Slams won from April 1968 – the start of the Open Era in tennis – up until the end of 2013.

BOOKER PRIZE

We are looking for the name of any writer who has won the Booker/Man Booker Prize for Fiction before they turned forty, from its inception up to and including the prize awarded in 2013.

US PRESIDENTS

BARACK OBAMA	61
BILL CLINTON	39
FRANKLIN PIERCE	0
GROVER CLEVELAND	0
JAMES A. GARFIELD	0
JAMES K. POLK	0
JOHN F. KENNEDY	50
THEODORE ROOSEVELT	0
ULYSSES S. GRANT	0

TENNIS GRAND SLAM

ARANTXA SÁNCHEZ VICARIO	0
BJÖRN BORG	6
BORIS BECKER	29
CHRIS EVERT	6
EVONNE GOOLAGONG CAWLEY	7
IVA MAJOLI	0
MARIA SHARAPOVA	10
MARTINA HINGIS	9
MATS WILANDER	0
MICHAEL CHANG	0
MONICA SELES	0
PETE SAMPRAS	1
RAFAEL NADAL	6
SERENA WILLIAMS	11
STEFAN EDBERG	0
STEFFI GRAF	13
SVETLANA KUZNETSOVA	0
TRACY AUSTIN	7

BOOKER PRIZE

ARAVIND ADIGA	0	KERI HULME	0
ARUNDHATI ROY	0	KIRAN DESAI	0
BEN OKRI	0	RODDY DOYLE	0
ELEANOR CATTON	0	SALMAN RUSHDIE	2
J.G. FARRELL	0	V.S. NAIPAUL	0
KAZUO ISHIGURO	0	YANN MARTEL	0

Zachary Zaltzman, a zoophagous zealot, zizzes on a ziggurat while a zalophus zooms off on a zimmer.

Zayn – I write this with one hand as I am desperately fanning my eyes with the other to keep the tears from streaming down my face. But no, it's no good, I'll just have to give in to the flow. Actually, that *is* better, as my typing is much quicker now, although . . . yup there we go, just had to stop and blow my nose there. Aaanyway, where was I? Ah yes. Since the start of One Direction, *Pointless* has made no secret of its unabashed devotion to the band (although at the beginning we did hedge our bets a bit with The Wanted) and therefore has felt entitled to follow their progress towards world domination with an ever-so-slightly proprietary interest.

We all have our favourite 1D member of course and, when quizzed, Richard was always the first to say his was Zayn. In fact I rather think the whole Zayn Thing started on the floor of *Pointless* (by which I mean that the beat of the butterfly's wing that begat that hurricane happened 'during a recording of *Pointless*', not literally that something odd took place on the suspiciously shiny floor of the studio). With Richard nailing his colours so boldly to the Zayn mast, countless thousands of other fans felt the stirrings and realised that they too wanted to proclaim their love of the Malik. In fact, now I think about it Richard could well be responsible for the mania (the Zaynia) that in fact eventually drove Malik *from* the band. The pressure of having to live up to Osman's endorsement was at times too much for those young shoulders to bear, I imagine. Obviously this is pure conjecture; it's entirely possible that Richard may *not* be the only reason Zayn decided to walk but the message is clear: if you get the backing of the big guy, you've got to make sure you're ready for it.

My favourite is the Irish one with the face like a pie.

Zzzzz – Yes, it's definitely time to put the book down and turn off the light now. Ahhh *stretch* Haaaapy Chriiiistmas *yawn*. Tomorrow has so many excitements in store, *deeeeeep yaaaaawn* nnggmmm nnggmmm . . . you've got all those people coming round for lunch don't forget. You hadn't forgotten! Had you? Oh they'll be fine.

It's Christmas. Give 'em cold turkey and baked potatoes. Just as long as you haven't run out of booze. Goodnight! Zzzzzzzzz.

Actually, how are you for booze? 'Cos I don't think there's much beer left – that all went on Christmas Eve. There's always that bottle of Midori in the cupboard, but . . . ah well, let's worry about it in the morning shall we? Goodnight and sleep well and thank you for everything. Hope you enjoyed the book as much as we've enjoyed putting it together. *fiiiinal yaaaaaaaaaaaaaawn* Night night. Zzzzzzzzz.

Actually, I think Alison and David polished off that Midori last summer.

WORD ENDING IN 'ZZY'

We are looking for words that occur in the *Oxford English Dictionary* that end with the letters 'ZZY'. Any word with a hyphen anywhere in it (in the OED's spelling) does not count.

Proper nouns, and words marked 'offensive' by the dictionary, will not be counted.

BIZZY	9	NAZZY	0
BUZZY	10	POZZY	0
DIZZY	62	QUIZZY	1
FIZZY	58	SCUZZY	12
FRIZZY	6	SHOWBIZZY	0
FUZZY	19	SNAZZY	0
HUZZY	0	TIZZY	16
JAZZY	17	WHIZZY	9
MIZZY	1	WUZZY	2
MOZZY	1	ZAZZY	1
MUZZY	5	ZIZZY	2

FAMOUS NEW ZEALANDERS

We are going to show you a set of clues to fourteen famous people who were born in New Zealand. Their initials appear in brackets after each clue. We'd like you to work out who they are and tell us the one you think the fewest of our 100 people knew.

Actress turned psychologist, married to Billy Connolly (PS)

Country musician who married Nicole Kidman in 2006 (KU)

Director of the *Lord of the Rings* and *Hobbit* films (PJ)

Knighted cricketer who has taken most Test wickets for NZ (RH)

Lead singer of 'Crowded House' (NF)

Mountaineer who reached the summit of Everest in 1953 (EH)

Oscar-winning comedy partner of Jemaine Clement in *Flight of the Conchords* (BM)

FAMOUS NEW ZEALANDERS

Physicist whose name was given to an element and a unit of radioactivity (ER)

Played 'Jim Robinson' in the soap opera *Neighbours* (AD)

Played the title role in *Xena: Warrior Princess* (LL)

Rugby-player, who in 1994 became the youngest-ever capped All Black (JL)

Singer who had a UK number one hit with 'Gotta Get Thru This' (DB)

Star of the films *Gladiator* and *A Beautiful Mind* (RC)

The country's female Prime Minister 1999–2008 (HC)

ERNEST RUTHERFORD	1
ALAN DALE	20
LUCY LAWLESS	14
JONAH LOMU	16
DANIEL BEDINGFIELD	33
RUSSELL CROWE	62
HELEN CLARK	0

'Z' LIST

We're going to give you clues to five people whose surnames begin with 'Z'. We want you to identify them and, as ever, tell us the most obscure.

American director who won an Academy Award for his work on *Forrest Gump* (1994)

Born Paul Collins, British magician who was a pioneer of street magic on TV

French footballer who won FIFA world player of the year three times

---

French novelist who wrote *Germinal* (1885)

US musician who recorded his debut album in 1966 with 'The Mothers of Invention'

RENÉE ZELLWEGER FILMS

We are looking for the title of any film made for general cinema release, prior to the end of 2011, for which Renée Zellweger receives an acting credit according to IMDb. Short films, TV films and documentaries will not count, but voice performances will.

8 SECONDS	1	LEATHERHEADS	1
A PRICE ABOVE RUBIES	0	LIAR	0
APPALOOSA	0	LOVE AND A .45	0
BEE MOVIE	0	ME, MYSELF & IRENE	8
BRIDGET JONES: THE EDGE OF REASON	10	MISS POTTER	3
BRIDGET JONES'S DIARY	26	MONSTERS VS ALIENS	2
CASE 39	2	MY ONE AND ONLY	1
CHICAGO	12	MY OWN LOVE SONG	0
CINDERELLA MAN	1	NEW IN TOWN	1
COLD MOUNTAIN	7	NURSE BETTY	3
DOWN WITH LOVE	5	ONE TRUE THING	0
EMPIRE RECORDS	1	REALITY BITES	0
JERRY MAGUIRE	9	SHARK TALE	2
		THE BACHELOR	0